D1596066

WITHDRAWN FROM
MACALESTER COLLEGE
LIBRARY

Asian/Oceanian Historical Dictionaries
Edited by Jon Woronoff

Asia
1. *Vietnam,* by William J. Duiker. 1989
2. *Bangladesh,* by Craig Baxter and Syedur Rahman. 1989
3. *Pakistan,* by Shahid Javed Burki. 1991
4. *Jordan,* by Peter Gubser. 1991
5. *Afghanistan,* by Ludwig W. Adamec. 1991
6. *Laos,* by Martin Stuart-Fox and Mary Kooyman. 1992
7. *Singapore,* by K. Mulliner and Lian The-Mulliner. 1991
8. *Israel,* by Bernard Reich. 1992
9. *Indonesia,* by Robert Cribb. 1992
10. *Hong Kong and Macau,* by Elfed Vaughan Roberts, Sum Ngai Ling, and Peter Bradshaw. 1992
11. *Korea,* by Andrew C. Nahm. 1993
12. *Taiwan,* by John F. Copper. 1993
13. *Malaysia,* by Amarjit Kaur. 1993
14. *Saudi Arabia,* by J. E. Peterson. 1993
15. *Myanmar,* by Jan Bečka. 1995
16. *Iran,* by John H. Lorentz. 1995
17. *Yemen,* by Robert D. Burrowes. 1995
18. *Thailand,* by May Kyi Win. 1995
19. *Mongolia,* by Alan J. K. Sanders. 1996
20. *India,* by Surjit Mansingh. 1996
21. *Gulf Arab States,* by Malcolm C. Peck. 1996
22. *Syria,* by David Commins. 1996
23. *Palestine,* by Nafez Y. Nazzal and Laila A. Nazzal. 1997
24. *Philippines,* by Artemio R. Guillermo and May Kyi Win. 1997

Oceania
1. *Australia,* by James C. Docherty. 1992
2. *Polynesia,* by Robert D. Craig. 1993
3. *Guam and Micronesia,* by William Wuerch and Dirk Ballendorf. 1994
4. *Papua New Guinea,* by Ann Turner. 1994
5. *New Zealand,* by Keith Jackson and Alan McRobie. 1996

New Combined Series
25. *Brunei Darussalam,* by D. S. Ranjit Singh and Jatswan S. Sidhu. 1997
26. *Sri Lanka,* by S. W. R. de A. Samarshinghe and Vidyamali Samarsinghe. 1997
27. *Vietnam,* 2nd ed., by William J. Duiker. 1997

28. *People's Republic of China: 1949–1997,* by Lawrence R. Sullivan, with the assistance of Nancy Hearst. 1997
29. *Afghanistan,* 2nd ed., by Ludwig W. Adamec. 1997
30. *Lebanon,* by As'ad AbuKhalil. 1997
31. *Azerbaijan,* by Tadeusz Swietochowski and Brian C. Collins. 1999
32. *Australia,* 2nd ed., by James C. Docherty. 1999
33. *Pakistan,* 2nd ed., by Shahid Javed Burki. 1999
34. *Taiwan (Republic of China),* 2nd ed., by John F. Copper. 1999

Historical Dictionary
of Azerbaijan

Tadeusz Swietochowski
and
Brian C. Collins

Asian/Oceanian Historical Dictionaries, No. 31

The Scarecrow Press, Inc.
Lanham, Maryland, & London
1999

SCARECROW PRESS, INC.

Published in the United States of America
by Scarecrow Press, Inc.
4720 Boston Way
Lanham, Maryland 20706

4 Pleydel Gardens, Folkstone
Kent CT20 2DN, England

Copyright © 1999 by Taduesz Swietochowski and Brian C. Collins

All rights reserved. No part of this publication may be reproduced,
stored in a retrieval system, or transmitted in any form or by any
means, electronic, mechanical, photocopying, recording, or otherwise,
without permission of the publisher.

British Library Cataloguing in Publication Information Available

Library of Congress Cataloging-in-Publication Data

Historical dictionary of Azerbaijan / Tadeusz Swietochowski and Brian C.
   Collins.
       p.   cm. — (Asian/Oceanian historical dictionaries ; no. 31)
    Includes bibliographical references.
    ISBN 0-8108-3550-9 (cloth : alk. paper)
    1. Azerbaijan—History—Dictionaries.   I. Swietochowski, Tadeusz,
1934–   .   II. Collins, Brian C., 1964–   .   III. Series.
DK693.7.H57   1999
947.54—dc21   98-36400
                                                                     CIP

♾ ™The paper used in this publication meets the minimum requirements of
American National Standard of Information Sciences—Permanence of
Paper for Printed Library Materials, ANSI Z39.48-1984.
Manufactured in the United States of America.

Contents

Editor's Foreword   *Jon Woronoff*   vii

Preface   ix

Chronology   xi

Map   xiv

Introduction   1

THE DICTIONARY   11

Bibliography   137

About the Author   145

Editor's Foreword

For most of its history, Azerbaijan has been part of somebody else's empire. Most recently and emphatically, it was part of the Union of Soviet Socialist Republics. It has also been dominated by the Medes, the Persians, and Alexander the Great and later Iran, the Arabs, and the Turks. What was defined geographically as Azerbaijan changed repeatedly. Yet through it all the Azeris preserved a distinct identity. Now, with the breakup of the USSR, they can again try to form a nation. This will not be simple, and recent results are patchy. Still, strategically located and of economic interest to others, Azerbaijan can no longer be overlooked.

Given its history, Azerbaijan is certainly not an easy country to describe. But this historical dictionary does an excellent job despite all of the difficulties. It provides numerous entries on persons, institutions, and events, emphasizing recent periods but looking all the way back to ancient times. There are others on important aspects of the economy, society, religion, and culture. The introduction offers a broad view of the country while the chronology helps the reader follow events through history. Because Azerbaijan has been neglected by Western scholars, written studies in English are rather few and must be supplemented by works in other languages, especially indigenous Azeri and Russian. So the bibliography, while modest in size, is especially important.

This *Historical Dictionary of Azerbaijan* was written by Tadeusz Swietochowski and Brian C. Collins. Dr. Swietochowski is a foreign specialist who for decades has been studying, teaching, lecturing, and writing on this part of the world. Of special note are his two books, *Russian Azerbaijan, 1905-1920: The Shaping of National Identity in a Muslim Community,* and *Russia and Azerbaijan: A Borderland in Transition.* His co-author, Brian C. Collins, is a writer and historian with an avid interest in Azerbaijan. All who are interested in this new and old country should appreciate their efforts.

Jon Woronoff
Series Editor

Preface

Until recently the name of Azerbaijan remained little known. Now it is increasingly coming to public attention worldwide, and we hope that this volume will be of use to interested readers. Azerbaijan's history is long and rich, so much so that the work of putting together the dictionary imposed inevitable choices, especially with regard to geographical and chronological scope. These are choices of emphasis rather than exclusion: a larger proportion of entries deals with the modern age, which in Azerbaijan covers the 19th and 20th centuries, following the conquest of the northern part of the country by the Soviet Union. Likewise, most of the entries deal with this region, which would become the territory of the present-day Republic of Azerbaijan.

In the category of entries that offer biographical information, we have generally not included living persons, on the assumption that they have not completed their achievements, even though their names might be mentioned in other entries. Yet there are exceptions to this pattern, most notably for the heads of the Azerbaijani state.

As in any work dealing with Azerbaijan's history, personal names have presented a problem. The very use of the family names was a feature attendant on Russian rule and typically names would take Russian endings. Yet changing circumstances have encouraged many individuals to assume native-sounding versions of family names, and such versions are for the most part used in the dictionary.

This work to a large extent has been based on our past research, and we have made use of our previously published results in books and scholarly articles.

Now that work has come to an end, we wish to express our thanks to all those who in various ways contributed to its completion—in particular, Greg Twyman and Peter Scott. Preparation of the manuscript was made possible with the Grant in Aid for Creativity awarded by Monmouth University, New Jersey.

Chronology

ca. 900–700 B.C.	Azerbaijan is a part of the Median Empire.
ca. 600–400 B.C.	Azerbaijan is part of the Persian Empire.
330 B.C.	Azerbaijan becomes a part of the empire of Alexander the Great.
328 B.C.	Azerbaijan under the rule of Alexander's satrap Atropat.
323 B.C.	Azerbaijan becomes a part of the Selucid Empire.
224 A.D.	Caucasian Albania becomes a vassal of Sassanid Iran.
ca. 600	The Sassanids create the state of Shirvan to protect their Caucasian frontier.
667	Caucasian Albania becomes a vassal of Arab Abbasid caliphate.
816–837	Babak's uprising against Arab rule.
ca. 1000	Influx of Oghuz Turks.
1410	Shirvan state becomes a vassal of the Qara-Qoyunlus.
1538	Safavid Iran annexes the Shirvan state.
1747	Assassination of Nadir Shah. Azerbaijan breaks up into independent khanates.
1801	Russia annexes Georgia.
1804–1812	First Russo-Iranian War.
1813	Treaty of Gulistan. Russia annexes a part of northern Azerbaijan.
1826–1828	Second Russo-Iranian War.
1828	Treaty of Turkmanchai. Russia completes the conquest of northern Azerbaijan.
1872	The Baku Oil Revolution begins.
1905–1907	The First Russian Revolution.
1906–1911	Iranian Constitutional Revolution.
1908	The Young Turkish Revolution.
1911	Musavat Party founded.

1917	Overthrow of the monarchy in Russia, February. Bolsheviks overthrow the Provisional Government, October.
1918	Transcaucasian Federation of Armenia, Georgia, and Azerbaijan is formed in April, dissolved in May. Azerbaijan declares its independence, May 28th.
1920	Overthrow of the Azerbaijani Democratic Republic, April 28. Beginning of Soviet rule.
1922	Transcaucasian Soviet Federated Socialist Republic (TSFSR) is formed.
1933	Mir Jafar Baghirov becomes the head of the Communist Party of Azerbaijan.
1936	TSFSR is dissolved. Azerbaijan becomes a union republic of the USSR.
1937	Stalin purge reaches high point.
1941–45	Soviet-German war. Red Army occupies Iranian Azerbaijan.
1945	Autonomous Government formed in Iranian Azerbaijan.
1946	Soviet withdrawal from Iran and the fall of the 1947 Autonomous Government.
1953	Baghirov is removed from position of leadership of the Communist Party of Azerbaijan. De-Stalinization campaign begins.
1969	Haidar Aliyev becomes the head of the Communist Party of Azerbaijan.
1983	Aliyev promoted to the Politburo in Moscow.
1988	Outbreak of Armenian-Azeri violence linked to the Nagorno-Karabagh dispute.
1989	Formation of the People's Front of Azerbaijan is completed. General strike in Baku (September).
1990	Baku "January Days." Ayaz Mutalibov takes over the leadership of the Communist Party of Azerbaijan.
1991	The Republic of Azerbaijan declares its independence from the Soviet Union.
1992	Ayaz N. Mutalibov resigns as the president of Azerbaijan in March. Abulfaz Elchibey is elected president of the Republic in June.
1993	Surat Huseynov's military coup removes Elchibey from the office in June. Haidar Aliyev is elected as his successor in August.

1994	Contract of the Century signed with the international consortium of oil companies (September). Attempted coup against Aliyev (October).
1995	Another coup attempt in March. Parliamentary elections in November won by the Aliyev party. New constitution is accepted in the referendum.
1997	First transport of oil through the pipeline to Novorossiysk, November. Elchibey returns to Baku from exile.
1998	Aliyev reelected as president.

Azerbaijan

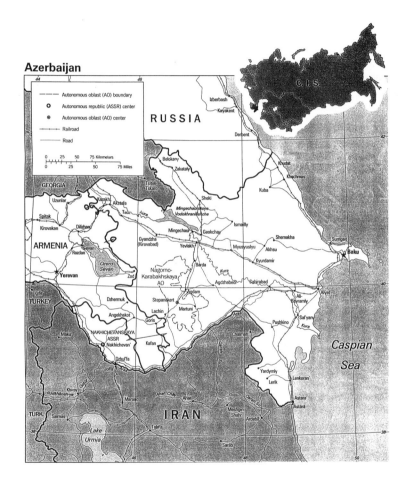

Autonomous oblast (AO) boundary

○ Autonomous republic (ASSR) center

◉ Autonomous oblast (AO) center

━┿━ Railroad

Road

0   25   50   75 Kilometers
0   25   50   75 Miles

RUSSIA

GEORGIA

ARMENIA

TURKEY

TURK.

IRAN

Nagorno-
Karabakhskaya
AO

NAKHICHEVANSKAYA
ASSR

**Caspian
Sea**

C.I.S.

Izberbash
Kayakent
Derbent
Khudat
Khachmas
Belokany
Zakataly
Tsiteli
Tskaro
Sheki
Kuba
Uzunlar
Kazakh
Akstafa
Toau
Mingechaurskoye
Vodokhranilishche
Ismailly
Spitak
Dilizhan
Kirovakan
Gyandzha
(Kirovabad)
Mingechaur
Geokchay
Shemakha
Sumgait
Razdan
Sevan
Yevlakh
Myusyuslyu
Akhsu
Baku
Ozero
Sevan
Barda
Kura
Kyurdamir
Yerevan
Zod
Agdzhabedi
Sabirabad
Dzhermuk
Stepanakert
Agdam
Ali-
Bayramly
Alyat
Lachin
Goris
Martuni
Aras
Pushkino
Sal'yany
Kura
Angekhakot
Maku
Kafan
Chalman
Kura
Nakhichevan'
Dzhul'fa
Jolfa
Yardymly
Lerik
Lenkoran'
Khvoy
Rudkhaneh-ye
Astara
Astārā
Salmas
Marand
Ahar Chay
Ahar
Qareh Su
Meshgin
Shahr
Ardebil
Tabriz
Lake
Urmia
Sarab

Introduction

Land and People

The land of Azerbaijan and its people are divided into two parts. One, extending north of the Araxes River in the geographical region of Transcaucasia, is today an independent state. The Republic of Azerbaijan covers 33,436 square miles (86,600 sq km) and includes the Nagorno-Karabagh Autonomous Oblast (NKAO) in the west (1,699 square miles or 4,400 sq km), as well as the noncontiguous Nakhichevan Autonomous State in the southwest (2,124 square miles or 5,500 sq km). The republic borders Russia in the north, Georgia in the northwest, Armenia in the southwest, Iran in the south, and the Caspian Sea in the east. The other part of Azerbaijan, south of the Araxes River, lies within the frontiers of Iran, and is known as Iranian Azerbaijan. The people on both sides of the border speak the same Azeri Turkish language, share the religion of Islam, and had a common history until the Russian conquest of northern Azerbaijan in the first half of the 19th century.

Nearly half of the Azerbaijani Republic's territory is covered by mountains, of which the highest is Bazarduizi Peak at 14,652 feet (4,466 m). The three main relief features of Transcaucasia converge within the country. These are the Greater Caucasus Mountains in the northeast, the Lesser Caucasus in the southwest, and the Kura River depression between them. In the extreme southeast are the Talysh Mountains, and the Araxes River stretches between the Zangezur and Dilagarez mountain ranges. The highest elevations are in the Greater Caucasus region, which abounds in glaciers and rapids. The middle-altitude ranges are broken by deep valleys. The Greater Caucasus drops off abruptly to the east and becomes arid hills. North of this range, in eastern Azerbaijan, extends the sloping Kusary Plateau. The lowest part of the country, the Kura River depression in the southeast, is divided into two sections. Its western area and northern rim are marked by hills, ridges, and valleys. The central and

1

eastern areas of the depression consist of alluvial flatland and the low delta of the Kura River along the coast. The 500-mile-long Caspian coastline has few irregularities. The largest projections are the Apsheron Peninsula, the Sara Peninsula, and the Kura Sandbar. The major waterways are the Araxes and Kura rivers. The rainfall averages 200–400 mm per year. In the south of the Azerbaijani Republic a subtropical climate prevails, and rainfall is sufficient for agriculture. Eighteen percent of the land is under cultivation, and 24 percent is pasture. Near the capital city of Baku lie extensive oil and gas deposits. The production of electrical energy averages about 3,250 kwh per capita. The rail lines total 1,296 miles (2,090 km) and highways 22,753 miles (36,699 km).

Azerbaijan's capital, Baku, is situated on the Apsheron Peninsula and is the largest city of the republic, containing about 25 percent of the country's population. It is a major Caspian Sea port and a center of the oil industry. The republic's second-largest city is Ganja, 198 miles (320 km) west of Baku.

Iranian Azerbaijan lies between the Caspian Sea coast, Lake Urmia, and the Araxes River. A part of the Islamic Republic of Iran, a majority of its population is Azeris, whose numbers in Iran are estimated at 15 million. Major cities in Iranian Azerbaijan are Tabriz, Ardabil, Zanjan, Khoi, and Maragin. The largest of them, Tabriz, is an important industrial center with a population of over 600,000.

The Azerbaijani Republic's population, including Nagorno-Karabagh, exceeds 7.5 million, of which about 85 percent are ethnic Azeris. The two largest non-Azeri groups in 1989 were Russians, 392,000 or 5.8 percent, and a similar number of Armenians.

History

As a political or administrative entity, and indeed as a geographic notion, Azerbaijan's confines were changing throughout history. Its northern part was known at times under different names; in the pre-Islamic period it was called Caucasian Albania, and, subsequently, Arran. From the time of ancient Media and the Achaemenid Kingdom, Azerbaijan shared its history with Iran. According to widely accepted etymology its name derives from Atropates, an Iranian satrap who remained in power under Alexander the Great and eventually established a dynasty of local rulers.

Azerbaijan shared its destinies with Iran, and maintained its Iranian character after the conquest by the Arabs in the mid-seventh century and its subsequent conversion to Islam. Only in the 11th century, with the influx of nomadic Oghuz tribes under the Seljuk dynasty, did the country acquire a significant proportion of Turkic-speaking inhabitants. The original population began to mix with immigrants, and the native idiom of the Iranian family of languages was gradually replaced by a dialect that evolved into a distinct Azeri-Turkish language.

The process of Turkification was long and uneven, sustained by successive waves of incoming nomads from Central Asia. After the Mongol invasions in the 13th century, Azerbaijan became a part of the empire of Hulagu and his successors, the Ilkhanids. Subsequently it passed under the rule of the Turkmen who founded the rival Aq-Qoyunlu and Qara-Qoyunlu states. The post-Mongol period brought the first flourishing of Azeri Turkish as a literary language that was used far beyond Azerbaijan, a process that culminated in the poetic works of such writers as Nesimi (d. 1418), Khatai (d. 1525), and Fuzuli of Baghdad (d. 1556).

At the end of the 15th century Azerbaijan became the power base of the native dynasty, the Safavids. Through a vigorous policy of expansion and consolidation they built a new Iranian Kingdom. Shah Ismail I (1501–1524) known also as a poet under the pen name Khatai, elevated the Shi'a branch of Islam to the status of the state religion of his empire, an act that reinforced its internal cohesion and set the Azeris firmly apart from the ethnically and linguistically close Ottoman Turks. Under the early Safavids their homeland was frequently the battleground in the wars between Iran and Sunni Turkey. Because of the threat of Ottoman incursions, the capital of Iran was moved from Tabriz to Qazvin, and then, under Abbas the Great (1588–1629), to Isfahan. A strategically vital province, Azerbaijan remained under the authority of a governor, who usually combined his administrative position with the highest military rank. Safavid rule, gradually shedding its Azeri character, lasted for more than two centuries. Undermined by internal strife and an Afghan invasion, it came to an end in 1722.

The second half of the 18th century saw a period of decline of central authority in Iran, a condition that allowed the emergence of indigenous centers of power in the Azerbaijan periphery. These took the form of khanates (principalities), including Karabagh, Baku, Shirvan, Ganja, Derbent, Kuba, Talysh, Nakhichevan, and Erivan in the northern part of the country, and Tabriz, Urumiyeh, Ardabil, Khoi, Maku, Karadagh, and Maragin in the south.

Political fragmentation led to internecine warfare among the khanates and also facilitated interference from outside powers, Turkey and Russia, which competed for domination over the region south of the Caucasus

Mountains. Toward the end of the century, as the Ottoman State sank deeper into decline, the shadow that Russia cast over Transcaucasia lengthened ominously.

Russia's interest in the land beyond the Caucasus was long-standing and had diverse motivations, but the overriding attraction was the strategic value of the isthmus between the Caspian and Black Seas. Russian military involvement dated back to the reign of Peter the Great (1682–1725), whose unsuccessful Iranian Expedition aimed at projecting the Russian presence in the direction of the Indian Ocean. The southward drive resumed in a more sustained and systematic manner under Catherine II (1762–1796), and Russia began to throw its weight into the politics of the Transcaucasian states, notably through extending its protection to the Christian rulers of Kakheti-Kartli and Imeretia. With time, hegemony turned into direct rule when Tsar Alexander I (1801–1825) proclaimed the creation of the *guberniia* (province) of Georgia, consisting of the lands of the former Kakheti-Kartli kings.

The Conquest by Russia and a Century of Tsarist Rule

To secure a strategic hold on Georgia, the Russian high command of the Caucasus extended its control over the Azerbaijani khanates eastward to the Caspian coast and southward to the Araxes River by imposing vassalage treaties. The Russian conquests met with a challenge from Iran, now recovered from its weakness under the new dynasty of the Turkmen Qajar tribe. There followed two Russo-Iranian wars, both of which Russia won. The first of the wars ended in the 1813 Treaty of Gulistan awarding Russia most of Azerbaijan north of the Araxes River. The second war (1826–1828) ended with the Treaty of Turkmanchai, completing the conquest and establishing the Araxes River as the boundary that permanently divides Azerbaijan in two.

During the two centuries that followed, under the tsarist empire and the Soviet system alike, Azerbaijan oscillated between three models of foreign rule: dependency, colony, and organic merger. Each of these models was related to the stakes that Russia had in the region, and the resources it was willing to commit. The dependency model reflected almost exclusively Russia's strategic interests in Azerbaijan as a corridor for the penetration of Iran and as a position from which to outflank Turkey. In practical terms, it amounted to the bare minimum of expenditure in funds and manpower. This meant that the government, administrative, and judicial powers were all left in native hands and that the khanate system remained essentially unchanged, even if a khan himself was replaced by a Russian military commander. The prevailing model, colonialism, consisted of a Russian administrative structure and top echelon local bureaucracy, yet it also featured implicit recognition of regional autonomy and ethnocultural identity.

In contrast, the organic merger aimed at the fullest possible integration with Russia, not only administratively, but also economically and culturally. Under this policy, Azerbaijan experienced rapid, if lopsided, industrialization focused on the extraction of oil and limited to the metropolitan area of Baku. The oil revolution in turn brought the influx of immigrants, mainly Russian and Armenian, accompanied by a growth in intercommunal tensions, which erupted in violence when the empire entered its period of crisis.

The Age of Revolution and Political Awakening

The Russian Revolution of 1905–1907 was closely followed by the Iranian Constitutional Revolution of 1906–1911 and the Young Turk Revolution of 1908. Each of these three upheavals left its impact on Azerbaijan and involved some Azeri participation. At home, bloody confrontations between Armenians and Azeris produced a feeling of unity above regional, sectarian, or kinship loyalties. The weakening of government controls made possible the flourishing of the Azeri language press, an intellectual ferment, and the rise of political associations. Of these, the **Musavat** (Equality) party, formed clandestinely in 1911, became the largest political force in Azerbaijan after the overthrow of the monarchy in Russia in February 1917, assuming the character of a liberal-secular, nationalist movement.

Experiment in Nation-State Independence

After the Bolshevik seizure of power in Petrograd, Transcaucasia refused to recognize the new regime and in the winter of 1918 formed a regional legislative body called the Seim (Diet). In the spring, the Seim proclaimed the creation of the Transcaucasian Federation consisting of Georgia, Armenia, and Azerbaijan. However, the attempt at regional federalism proved to be short-lived. The Federation broke up within four weeks of internal strife and external pressures from Turkey and Germany. On May 28, 1918, the Azerbaijani National Council declared the creation of the Azerbaijani Democratic Republic with the provisional capital in the city of Ganja. The hitherto seldom used term "Azerbaijan" became the name for the state of the people who had previously been called Tatars, Caucasian Turks, or Caucasian Muslims.

The Democratic Republic lasted 23 months. The period of its existence can be divided into three distinct phases. The first was that of the Ottoman occupation whose military authorities tended to regard Azerbaijan as a land to be one day united with Turkey. Ottoman occupation was replaced by the British whose forces arrived in Baku in November 1918. In the second phase the British presence provided Azerbaijan with temporary security from the conflagration of the Russian Civil War, and indirectly it encouraged the political development of the country along the lines of a parliamentary system of government.

The phase of full independence that followed the British withdrawal in August 1919 was clouded by a growing sense of insecurity and isolation. The survival of the Democratic Republic hinged on the stalemate in the civil war that would keep the Red and White Russian armies occupied far from Azerbaijan. By the spring of 1920 the Red Army had achieved victory, and on April 28 its troops invaded Azerbaijan, meeting with almost no resistance as the Azerbaijani forces were trying to put down an Armenian uprising in Nagorno-Karabagh. Before the end of the month the Azerbaijani Soviet of People's Commmissars was formed in Baku.

The Early Soviet Period

The new chapter in Azerbaijani history opened with the suppression of armed uprisings that kept breaking out in various parts of the country. With some degree of internal peace established, Azerbaijan, Georgia, and Armenia were once again united into a regional grouping, the Transcaucasian Soviet Federated Socialist Republic (*Zakfederatsiia*), which was jointly admitted to the Union of Soviet Socialist Republics.

The official Soviet policy toward non-Russian nationalities in the 1920s was *korenizatsiia* (nativization), under which the native element was to be given preference in appointments to positions in the government bureaucracy. The Azeri intelligentsia found it an opportunity to pursue some of its favorite programs of an enlightenment/educational nature. By the end of the decade, militant secularism had become the government policy, which soon led to excesses and brutalities. Although Islam was greatly weakened as a religion it retained much of its strength among the population as a way of life, with its traditional customs and prohibitions generally observed. The Soviet anti-Islamic drive and the collectivization campaign in the countryside were only the prelude for a more violent and all-encompassing upheaval in the 1930s.

Stalin's Great Terror and World War II

Few other Soviet republics suffered proportionately greater human losses than Azerbaijan through mass killings, deportations, and imprisonment in this period. A special target of the purges was the intelligentsia, as well as the old-guard native communists, especially those who had been active in the independent republic or had contacts with revolutionary movements in neighboring Muslim countries. Typical accusations were for the crime of Pan-Islamism, Pan-Turkism, Musavatism, or bourgeois nationalism, but these often served for settling personal, family, or clan accounts. The old-time communists were replaced by newcomers to the ruling elite, from the ranks of youth raised under the Soviet regime.

In the year before the purges reached their height, the Stalin Constitution of 1936 was declared. One of its effects was the dissolution of the Transcaucasian Federation, after which Azerbaijan, Armenia, and Georgia became constituent republics of the USSR. In tune with the restructuring of the Soviet Union, the republics were now discouraged from direct relations with each other. Azerbaijan had to shed any residual ties to the Turkic and Islamic world. The official name of its inhabitants now became Azerbaijanis instead of Azeri-Turks. Likewise the national language was to be called Azerbaijani instead of Turkish, Azeri-Turkish, or Azeri. The years of the great purges also marked the onset of a vigorous drive for assimilation to the Russian language and culture, an effort to reinforce Soviet unity in the face of the approaching Second World War. Although many Azeris fought well in the ranks of the Red Army, tens of thousands of prisoners of war joined the German forces.

At the onset of the war, inward-looking, isolationist Soviet Azerbaijani nationalism was faced with the ripple effects of the Soviet occupation of Iranian Azerbaijan. Under Soviet military rule, the revival of Azeri as the literary language (which had largely been supplanted by Persian) was promoted with the help of writers, journalists, and educators from north of the Araxes. In November 1945, with Soviet backing, an Autonomous Government was proclaimed in Tabriz under Sayyid Jafar Pishevari, the leader of the Azerbaijani Democratic Party. Cultural institutions and education in the native language blossomed throughout Iranian Azerbaijan, and speculations grew rife about a Greater Azerbaijan that might result from unification of the two parts of the country under the Soviet aegis.

As it turned out, the issue of Iranian Azerbaijan was an opening skirmish of the Cold War, and under American and British pressure, the occupation army was withdrawn. The central government of Iran recovered its control over Azerbaijan by the end of 1946, and the Democratic Party leaders took refuge across the Soviet border. Pishevari, who was never fully trusted by the Soviets, soon died under mysterious circumstances.

Imperial Stagnation and Decline

The death of Stalin in 1953 was followed by the "Khrushchev Thaw," a period of relaxation of controls over literature, scholarship, and even the press. On the other hand, the thaw brought a new anti-Islamic campaign, and then a new Russification drive under the *Sblizhenie* (Rapprochement) policy that was to lead to the eventual amalgamation of all peoples of the USSR into one Soviet nation.

During the 1960s, signs of a structural crisis in the Soviet colonial empire began to surface. The Azerbaijani oil industry lost its relative weight in the economy of the Soviet Union, partly because of the shift to other regions, and partly because of the depletion of the easily accessible, onshore oil fields. The decline of the oil industry led, in turn, to reduced investments in Azerbaijan by central planning in Moscow. In the 1960s Azerbaijan ranked lowest in productivity growth rate and economic output among all Soviet republics, but it retained a high rate of population increase. The rapidly growing mass of white-collar workers saw little chance for fulfillment of their expectations, and ethnic tensions between the Azeris and Armenians were reawakening.

In an attempt to deal with the deteriorating condition of Azerbaijan, Moscow appointed Haidar Aliyev the head of the Communist Party of Azerbaijan (CPAz) in 1969. Aliyev temporarily reversed the economic downdrift and promoted alternative industries to the extraction and refining of oil. He also consolidated the republic's ruling elite, which was now composed almost entirely of ethnic Azeris. The echoes of the Islamic revolution in neighboring Iran stimulated the process of a religious revival, to which the Soviet reply was the nationalist-sounding slogan "one Azerbaijan"—promoted in literature and scholarship rather than in political action.

Decolonization and Its Crises

Although Azerbaijan lagged behind neighboring republics in raising a dissident movement, with the violent renewal of ethnic antagonism it experienced a sudden political awakening, comparable to that of

1905–1907. The new epoch began in February 1988 when Armenia formally raised its own claim to Nagorno-Karabagh. The conflict revealed the unsuitability of the Communist Party as the champion of national interests, and in the spirit of *glasnost,* independent publications and associations began to emerge. Of the latter, the largest was the People's Front of Azerbaijan (PFAz), which by the autumn of 1989 seemed to be poised for a takeover of power from the tottering Communist Party. To forestall this prospect, Soviet troops were dispatched to Baku, ostensibly to restore order after anti-Armenian riots in January 1990. The end of the regime came formally with the breakup of the USSR and the declaration of Azerbaijan's independence on August 30, 1991.

The Second Independent Republic

Among the issues facing the newborn Republic of Azerbaijan was the Nagorno-Karabagh conflict, which had grown into a prime national concern. The inability to deal with the war brought down the first president of independent Azerbaijan, ex-Communist Party leader Ayaz Mutalibov, in 1992. The same justification served as a pretext to overthrow his successor, democratically elected president Abulfaz Elchibey of the People's Front of Azerbaijan, in a military coup of June 1993.

The geopolitical aspect of oil deposits became an additional dimension of post-Soviet instability in Azerbaijan, its ramifications overshadowing the ethnic strife. The agreement with a consortium of Western companies on exploration of the rich Azerbaijani offshore oil fields displeased Moscow, and was seen as the deeper cause for the overthrow of the Elchibey regime by a military coup. His successor, former Communist leader Haidar Aliyev, renegotiated the oil agreement in 1994 and soon saw himself threatened by a series of attempted coups and separatist movements among ethnic minorities, the Lesgins and Talyshis, in addition to the Karabagh Armenians. His reply was strong-arm government policy, although tolerance for opposition groups was maintained.

To the present time, the crucial decisions concerning the routing of oil pipelines have not been finalized—a situation fraught with more upheavals in the future. While Russia remains the main geopolitical fact of Azerbaijan, economic interests bring Azerbaijan closer to the world oil markets. At the same time, its ethnicity, Islamic religion, history, and cultural traditions work toward restoration of its links with the Middle Eastern environment in general, and its special-relationship countries, Iran and Turkey, in particular.

THE DICTIONARY

-A-

ABBAS I, SHAH (1571–1629). A shah of the **Safavid dynasty (1588–1629)**, known also as Abbas the Great, he assumed the throne of Iran at the age of 17. After consolidating his rule, Abbas crushed the power of the **Qizilbash** aristocracy. He then used the wealth he acquired from confiscated properties of the Qizilbashis to build a standing army, which drove from Iran first the Uzbegs, then the Ottomans, recapturing from them Kars, and the Azerbaijani regions of **Tabriz,** and **Erivan.** In another campaign, in 1623, he recaptured from the Ottomans Baghdad, Shirvan, and Kurdistan. By the time of his death in 1629, Shah Abbas had restored to Iran the territories held at the time of **Ismail I.** He transferred the capital from Qazvīn to Isfahan, turning it into a thriving center of arts, craft-based industry, and commerce. *See also* QIZILBASH; SAFAVIDS.

ADALAT (JUSTICE). A Social Democratic organization of Iranian immigrants in **Baku,** formed in 1916. Among its founding members were Asadullah Gafarzade, Bahram Aghazade, Agha Baba Yusifzade, and the youthful Javadzade Khalkali, who was later to become famous as Jafar **Pishevari.** Adalat saw itself as the successor of the **Ejtima-i Amiyyun,** an organization active in the years 1906–1909. Adalat cooperated closely with the **Himmat Party,** and some members of the two organizations served on the central committees of both. It joined the **Muslim Socialist Bureau** under the **Baku Commune,** and in 1920 was absorbed by the **Communist Party of Azerbaijan** and the Communist Party of Iran. *See also* EJTIMA-I AMIYYUN; HIMMAT PARTY; MUSLIM SOCIALIST BUREAU.

11

AGHAMALIOGHLI, SAMAD AGHA (1867–1930). A prominent figure of political and intellectual life of Azerbaijan in the age of revolution. In the years 1918–1920, he was the head of the Menshevik wing of the **Himmat** and represented the party in the parliament, where he endorsed the Bolshevik takeover. Subsequently, he joined the **Communist Party of Azerbaijan**, and held high, if largely ceremonial, government positions. He gained fame for his supervision of the replacement of the Arabic alphabet with Latin, a change which he saw as a cultural revolution. *See also* ALPHABET REFORM.

AGHAYEV (AGAOGLU), AHMAD BEY (1865–1939). A prominent journalist and political activist in late 19th- and early-20th-century Azerbaijan. Aghayev received his university education in Paris, where he contributed to the French press. His early writings displayed a pro-Iranian and anti-Ottoman bias, and he originally looked toward Iran for leadership of the Muslim world. After his return to Azerbaijan in 1895 he began his evolution toward **Pan-Turkism,** which was evident in his articles in the Russian-language **Baku** newspaper *Kaspii* **(The Caspian),** and the **Young Turkish Revolution** of 1908, he moved to Istanbul, where he held middle-echelon government positions while continuing his journalistic work in the Ottoman newspapers. In the summer of 1918 he was appointed adviser to the Ottoman commander of the **Army of Islam,** Nuri Pasha. He remained in Baku after the withdrawal of Ottoman forces in the fall of 1918. The next year he was included in the Azeri delegation to the Versailles Peace Conference. However, while traveling to Paris, he was arrested in Istanbul by the British authorities, who regarded him as too closely linked to the leaders of the emerging nationalist movement in Turkey. After his release from detention in Malta, he returned to Turkey where he remained for the rest of his life. *See also* PRESS.

AKHUNDOV, MIRZA FATH ALI. *See* AKHUNDZADE (AKHUNDOV), MIRZA FATH ALI.

AKHUNDOV, VELI YUSIFOGHLI. Originally trained as a medical doctor, Akhundov was minister of health in the **Azerbaijani Soviet Socialist Republic** until 1958. He was abruptly promoted to chairman of the Council of Ministers, and then in 1959 became first secretary of the **Communist Party of Azerbaijan,** replacing Imam Dashdamiroghlu **Mustafayev.** Under his rule Azerbaijan experienced widespread corruption and the economy stagnated. Because of his mismanagement of the economy, Akhundov was replaced as first secretary in 1969 by Haidar **Aliyev.** After his fall from power, Akhundov was relegated to the position of vice president of the Azerbaijani Academy of Sciences.

AKHUNDZADE (AKHUNDOV), MIRZA FATH ALI (1812–1878). Azeri writer and philosopher, regarded as the founder and foremost representative of modern, native language **literature.** In the 1850s he wrote a series of comedies satirizing social ills rooted in ignorance and superstition, thus gaining the reputation as the "Moliére of the Orient" and becoming the pioneer of theater in the Turkic-speaking world and Iran. In his later philosophical writings he showed himself as a thinker combining rationalist traditions of the Middle East with European enlightenment. He crusaded for the spread of education and an end to religious fanaticism. With an eye on the current condition of Iran, he advocated reforms in the spirit of European liberalism, constitutionalism, and secularism. He exerted a major influence on 19th-century Iranian writers of a reformist disposition.

Concerned about the low level of literacy in Islamic countries, Akhundzade campaigned for the simplification of the Arabic alphabet, and eventually called for its replacement by the Latin. Although he identified himself with Iran, Akhundzade, by reinvigorating the native language literature, is recognized as a major force in the 19th-century movement for the self-assertion of Azeri cultural identity. *See also* ALPHABET REFORM; LITERATURE, AZERI.

AKINCHI. A 19th-century Muslim Left social revolutionary organization in **Baku** led by Ruhullah Akhundov. Its press organ was the newspaper *Akinchi* **(Ploughman)**. It became part of the **Muslim Socialist Bureau** under the Baku Sovnarkom and was eventually absorbed by the **Communist Party of Azerbaijan.** *See also* COMMUNIST PARTY OF AZERBAIJAN; MUSLIM SOCIALIST BUREAU.

AKINCHI **(PLOUGHMAN).** The first Azeri-language newspaper, published from July 22, 1875, to September 1877 in **Baku.** Its founder and editor in chief was Hasan bey **Zardabi,** a Moscow-educated Sunnite from Azerbaijan, who was influenced by the contemporary ideas of Russian populism (*Narodnichestvo*). The newspaper was controversial among Transcaucasian Muslims since many Shi'ite *ulama* (clergymen) considered it improper to imitate such an infidel invention as a newspaper. Others objected to the use of Azeri rather than Persian, the generally accepted literary idiom in Azerbaijan.

As *Akinchi* was designed to reach the Azeri peasant, it contained much material on agriculture and was written in a simple style with few Persian or Arabic words. Since the paper was rejected by the Shi'ite scholars and inaccessible to the mostly illiterate peasantry, *Akinchi* became a forum for the emerging Azeri **intelligentsia.** The newspaper was friendly toward Turkey, mildly critical of Iran, and inclined toward secularism. Among the Azeri intelligentsia, it had a considerable impact on the development of social, political, and artistic thought. *Akinchi* was closed down by the Russian authorities during the Russo-Turkish War of 1877 due to its perceived pro-Ottoman sympathies. *See also* ZARDABI, HASAN BEY; INTELLIGENTSIA.

ALBANIA. *See* CAUCASIAN ALBANIA.

ALI MUHAMMAD, SAYYID (d. 1852). An Iranian merchant-saint, who founded the religious-social Babist movement in the 1840s after proclaiming himself the *Bab* (gateway) to the Hidden Imam, the only true sovereign in the Shi'ite doctrine. His call for the safeguarding of freedoms, defense of private property from taxation and confiscation by the government, and provincial rights over the rights of the central government, found strong support in Iranian Azerbaijan, especially among the economically suffering merchants and craftsmen of **Tabriz.** In 1848 **Babism** openly seceded from Islam, and among the disturbances caused by its growing militancy was the 1850 uprising in Zanjān against Shah Nasr ul-Din. By 1852 the movement was brutally suppressed following the execution of Sayyid Ali Muhammad. *See also* BABISM.

ALIYEV, HAIDAR ALI RZAOGLI (1923–). Born in **Nakhichevan** on May 10, 1923, he served in **World War II.** He graduated from the Azerbaijani State University in the field of history in 1957. Within the Soviet security organization, KGB, he reached the rank of major-general. In 1969, Aliyev replaced Veli **Akhundov** as first secretary of the **Communist Party of Azerbaijan** in 1969, and held this post until the end of 1982. During his tenure in office he concentrated on cleaning up government corruption and improving the condition of the Azerbaijani economy. He also ethnically consolidated the ruling elite of Azerbaijan by appointing primarily Azeris to high positions. On the basis of his performance he was promoted by Iurii Andropov in 1983 to membership in the politburo of the Communist Party in Moscow, the highest position an Azeri had ever held in the USSR. He later served under Mikhail Gorbachev as deputy prime minister of the Soviet Union until his ouster in 1987.

Having fallen from favor in Moscow, Aliyev returned to Nakhichevan, where he ran unopposed in the 1990 parliamentary elections, receiving 95 percent of the vote. He became the head of the **Nakhichevan Autonomous Soviet Socialist Republic (ASSR)** Soviet and in this capacity conducted negotiations with Armenia, Iran, and Turkey.

Aliyev made his comeback to the center stage of Azerbaijani politics during the June 1993 military rebellion of Surat **Huseynov.** He was brought to **Baku** to replace Isa Gambar as the speaker of the **Azerbaijani National Council.** Then, after Abulfaz **Elchibey** left the capital, he became the acting president of the Republic. He was elected to the presidency by popular vote in October 1993. His second period at the helm of the Azerbaijani power structure has appeared as a stron-man rule with various degrees of tolerance toward the opposition. In the **Nagorno-Karabagh dispute,** the conclusion of the May 1994 cease-fire agreement helped him to consolidate his hold over the country.

In foreign policy Aliyev made the transition from Communist leader to Azerbaijani nationalist. Although one of his first steps was to bring Azerbaijan back to the CIS (Commonwealth of Independent States), he did not agree to the stationing of Russian troops in its territory.

Contracts signed since 1994 with Western companies for large-scale exploration of oil resources planted the seeds for Azerbaijan's increasingly pro-Western foreign policy. Furthermore, although Aliyev avoided antagonizing Moscow and, in fact, recognized Russia's geopolitical interest in the region, he faced a series of attempted coups, inspired by Russia to dislodge him from power. In response, there followed an increase in the number of political prisoners, as well as difficulties affecting the opposition parties and communication media.

This course of hard-line policy was relaxed after the November 1995 parliamentary elections in which Aliyev's New Azerbaijan Party won 70 percent of the vote. In October 1998, the year of his 75th birthday, Aliyev was reelected president of the republic by more than three quarters of the vote, but the results were hotly contested by opposition parties. *See also* COMMUNIST PARTY OF AZERBAIJAN; REPUBLIC OF AZERBAIJAN.

ALPHABET REFORM. As did all Islamic peoples, the **Azeris** used the Arabic script from the time of their acceptance of Islam in the seventh century. The Arabic alphabet was, however, ill suited to the phonetics of the Turkic languages, and, with the growing need for social communications in the 19th century, it came to be regarded as the main cause for widespread illiteracy among the population. The issue of alphabet reform was first raised by Mirza Fath Ali **Akhundzade,** who proposed including signs for vowels in the Arabic script. He journeyed to Istanbul to present his ideas to the Ottoman Scientific Society, but his project was rejected. Later, he proposed replacing the Arabic alphabet with Latin characters. Other projects followed, including those by Mammad Agha **Shahtakhtinski,** the publisher of the newspaper, *Sharq-i Rus* (The Russian East), which promoted the use of Azeri as the literary language together with alphabet reform. This call for reform was echoed by the recommendations of the 1906 Baku Teachers Convention, and the proposals that came during the period of the Democratic Republic. Only under the Soviet regime were the circumstances right for a radical solution. In 1922, the Communist leader Nariman **Narimanov** appointed an ardent advocate of Latinization, Samad Agha **Aghamalioghli,** the head of the commission for alphabet reform. The same year, a newspaper *Yeni yol* (The New Road) began its publication in Latin characters.

The issue of the reform soon turned into a bitter controversy, and Latinization was opposed not only by traditionalists defending the continuity of historical heritage, but also by the revolutionary-minded followers of the Tatar Communist Sultan Galiyev throughout the Soviet Union. In their eyes, the Arabic alphabet, by not marking vowels, kept alive the notion of one literary idiom for all Turkic peoples by blurring phonetic peculiarities of diverse dialects, and even languages. As for Moscow, it continued its usual policy of encouraging national differentiation among Muslims. Lenin gave his blessings to Aghamalioghli, and the reform went ahead in successive stages. On June 27, 1924, the administration of the **Azerbaijani SSR** began the official use of the Latin alphabet.

The question of the new alphabet dominated the First Soviet Turkology Congress that met in **Baku** in February 1926. The Congress recommended that other Turko-Tatar republics study the Azeri experience for the Latinization of their respective alphabets. The problem of Latinization soon transcended the purely Soviet-Turkic concern and aroused the interest of the Kemalist regime in Turkey. Somewhat quickly and without intermediate stages, Turkey adopted the new alphabet in November 1928 and banned the use of the Arabic alphabet from the new year on.

In Azerbaijan, alphabet reform gave a new momentum to the drive against illiteracy, and the results were impressive. The literacy ratio, which was 25.2 percent in 1926 rose to 31.4 percent in 1931, and 50.9 percent in 1933. By this time, the law on compulsory **education** had taken effect.

The use of the Latin alphabet came to an end with the policies of the Stalinist period aimed at isolating the Azeris from other Turkic peoples and forging a new Soviet nation through "implicit linguistic" Russification. In 1940 there came a new alphabet reform, the second in little more than a decade. This time, Cyrillic was adopted as the official alphabet. Unlike in the 1920s, there were no heated controversies, only endless acclamations in public meetings.

The unraveling of the Soviet Union again brought into public debate the need for a new alphabet reform. While there was a consensus that Cyrillic should be rejected as a symbol of Stalinist-imposed Russification and a barrier that had cut off the Azeris from the world outside the USSR, the question remained: should Azerbaijan restore the Latin alphabet of the 1920s? Or should it return to the Arabic script, a change that would bring unification with the Azeris in Iran, while restoring the continuity of Azerbaijan's historical and literary heritage. As the possibility of using the written Azeri **language** in Iran remained limited, it was "not worth the sacrifice" to bring back the Arabic script with all of its shortcomings. In January 1993, Azerbaijan adopted its fourth alphabet in less than 70 years, a Latin version more simplified than that of the 1920s, the reason for simplification being the requirements of the computer age. *See also* EDUCATION; JADIDISM.

AMOGHLI, HAIDAR KHAN (1880–1921). A prominent revolutionary whose activities spanned **Transcaucasia,** Iran, and Central Asia. Born to an immigrant Iranian Azeri family, he grew up in **Ganja.** As a student of the Tbilisi Polytechnic he became familiar with socialism, and then moved to Iran to work as an engineer in Mashhad. During the constitutional movement, he established a branch of the **Ejtima-i Amiyyun** in Teheran, an Iranian Social Democrat organization founded among the Iranian immigrants in Transcaucasia. Haider Khan's (he was not known under his last name) terrorist activities in defense of the constitution after the 1908 coup gained him the nickname *Bombi* (Bomber). In the second phase of the constitutional movement, together with M. A. **Rasulzade,** he joined the moderate Democratic Party. Exiled in 1912, he lived mainly in Istanbul, and during **World War I** he fought in the Ottoman-sponsored *Mujahidin-i Azarbaijan* (Fighters of Azerbaijan) military unit, and worked with the Iranian Committee in Berlin.

After the October Revolution in Russia (1917), Haidar Khan made his way to Russia, and then to Central Asia, where he was active in the **Adalat** Party among Iranian immigrants. Within the newly founded Communist Party of Iran, he belonged to the moderate wing, and in September 1920 became the head of the Central Committee. The next year, he moved to Gīlān, where he was made the commissar of foreign affairs in the Jangali-Communist coalition government of Kuchuk Khan, and was assassinated by the latter's followers. *See also* IRANIAN CONSTITUTIONAL REVOLUTION; RASULZADE.

APSHERON PENINSULA. A peninsula located on the western shore of the **Caspian Sea.** It extends 40 miles into the Caspian and is up to 20 miles wide. The capital city of **Baku** is located on the southern portion of the peninsula. It is a center of the **oil industry** and contains rich deposits of oil and natural gas. *See also* CASPIAN SEA.

AQ-QOYUNLU (WHITE SHEEP). A tribal league of nomadic **Oghuz Turks** centered around the region of Diyarbakir during the 14th and 15th centuries. The name was shared by the dynasty that headed the league. In the 15th century the Aq-Qoyunlu crushed the Qara-Qoyunlu (Black sheep) state and conquered Azerbaijan, Armenia, western Iran, and Iraq. Their capital was the city of **Tabriz.** The state became a powerful entity, which entered into alliance with Venice, the Pope, and Hungary against the Ottoman Turks in 1463. Due to weaknesses caused by internal dissension, the Aq-Qoyunlu were defeated at the beginning of the 16th century by the **Qizilbash** led by Ismail Safavid. *See also* QIZILBASH; SAFAVID DYNASTY.

ARAXES (ARAS) RIVER. Flowing through **Transcaucasia,** the Araxes River is 643 miles (1,060 km) long. It rises in Turkey on the slopes of

Mt. Bingol and forms the southern border of the **Nakhichevan Autonomous Soviet Socialist Republic** and part of the southern border of Azerbaijan before emptying into the **Kura River.** As the boundary between Iran and the Russian Empire, the Araxes has become the symbol of the division of Azerbaijan into two parts.

ARMENIANS IN AZERBAIJAN. For a few centuries prior to the Russian conquest, the main concentration of Armenians in Azerbaijan was in **Nagorno-Karabagh,** the mountainous part of the **Karabagh Khanate.** The Armenian presence in other parts of Azerbaijan rose dramatically following the Russian conquest in the first half of the 19th century. Immigration into Azerbaijan was primarily from Turkey and Iran following the treaties of **Turkmanchai** and Adrianople. With a view to encouraging the influx of Armenians, Tsar Nicholas I (1825–1855) decreed the formation of an Armenian *oblast'* (district) comprising the territories of the khanates of **Erivan** and **Nakhichevan.** Generally, the Tsarist regime tended to favor the Christian Armenians at the expense of the Muslim Azeris, especially in the local government and elective city councils, the *dumas.* The Muslim representation in these bodies was limited to one-third of the deputies. The oil boom of the late 19th century brought an influx of Armenians to **Baku,** largely from Nagorno-Karabagh. The Armenian population of the city doubled from 1897 to 1913, while the **Azeri** population grew only slightly. The Armenians in the **oil industry** tended to hold better-paying positions, while the native Muslims prevailed in the low-paying manual labor jobs.

Economic disparities as well as the depression in the oil industry were part of the backdrop for eruptions of ethnic violence on a mass scale from 1905 to 1907. The year 1918 was another period of mass violence, marked by the Armenian massacre of the Azeris in Baku in March, and the Azeri revenge in September.

The Soviet regime imposed intercommunal peace by force, and the policy of **korenizatsiia** (nativization) diminished Azeri fears of Armenian power in local politics and government. With the passage of time, as the great age of Baku oil was reaching its twilight, the incentives that had attracted immigrants were no longer present. The reverse process began—a slow but steady exodus of Armenians and Russians from Azerbaijan, noticeable since 1959. For the Armenians, an additional cause for out-migration was historical antipathy between them and the Azeris. From 1970 to 1979 the Armenian population of Azerbaijan decreased by 82,000.

By 1998 the Armenian population of Azerbaijan was 180,678, or 2.3 percent of the republic's total. A new wave of ethnic violence sparked by the **Nagorno-Karabagh dispute** has resulted in the emigration of Armenians from predominantly Azeri areas, and the flight of Azeris from Armenian areas. Nagorno-Karabagh is currently the largest Armenian enclave, with approximately 150,000 Armenians living in the district. *See also* NAGORNO-KARABAGH DISPUTE.

ARMY OF ISLAM. An Ottoman-Azeri-Daghestani military unit active in the latter stages of **World War I.** As part of the treaty of friendship signed by the **Azerbaijani Democratic Republic** and the Ottoman Empire in June 1918, this unit was raised within Azerbaijan with the avowed purpose of aiding **Azeri** self-defense against attacks by **Armenian** irregulars. The Army of Islam consisted of 7,000 Azeri and Caucasian irregulars and 8,000 Ottoman regulars under the command of Enver Pasha's younger half brother, Nuri Pasha. This unit, augmented by other Ottoman forces, defeated the troops of the Baku Soviet at Geokchai and took part in the seizure of **Baku** from the British on September 15, 1918, allowing the government of the Azerbaijani Democratic Republic to move to the capital.

Following the signing of the Mudros Armistice (October 9, 1918) ending Ottoman participation in World War I, the unit was disbanded. With the Ottoman evacuation of Azerbaijan, most of the Azeri irregulars and some of the Ottoman regulars joined the army of the Azerbaijani Democratic Republic. *See also* AZERBAIJANI DEMOCRATIC REPUBLIC.

ARRAN. Name given by Arab authors to the terrritory roughly conciding with Caucasian Albania. Arab sources of the 9th–10th centuries describe Arran as the region centered between the rivers **Araxes** and **Kura.** In subsequent centuries, the name "Arran" was used to describe territory of today's Azerbaijan north of the Araxes River.

ATROPATENE. A state in southern (Iranian) Azerbaijan which emerged in the fourth century B.C. and lasted until about 150 B.C. The territory derived its name from Atropates, a satrap of Alexander the Great appointed in 328 B.C. It is possible that the name of Azerbaijan is derived from Atropates.

AUTONOMOUS GOVERNMENT OF AZERBAIJAN. A regional authority established in Iranian Azerbaijan by the **Democratic Party of Azerbaijan** (DPAz) shortly after **World War II,** with Soviet backing. Since August 1941, the Red Army had occupied the region and given support to local far left organizations, such as the Tudeh Party and the DPAz, and helped the latter to seize power in Azerbaijan. On November 20, 1945, the DPAz, led by Jafar Sayyid **Pishevari,** convened the Constituent Congress in **Tabriz,** which declared Azerbaijan to be an autonomous entity, and addressed a proclamation to the shah and the Majlis of Iran and the governments of the United States, USSR, Great Britain, and France, stating that "the people of Azerbaijan have been endowed by history with distinct national, linguistic, cultural, and traditional characteristics which entitle them to freedom and autonomy." The proclamation affirmed that "the nation of Azerbaijan has no desire to separate itself from Iran or to harm the territorial integrity of Iran . . . and supports, with all its might, democracy, which in Iran takes a form of a constitutional government; it will participate in the functioning of the central government by electing deputies to the Majlis and by paying taxes." At the same time, the nation of Azerbaijan "officially and openly" asserted the right to form its own government and to "administer its internal and national affairs, respecting the integrity of Iran."

The National Congress to be convened would "elect the ministers for the Autonomous Government of Azerbaijan. The declaration emphasized a special attachment that "the nation of Azerbaijan has to its national and mother language. . . . The imposition of another language on the people of Azerbaijan has hindered their historical progress." The Congress therefore recommended that the Azeri language should be used in schools and government offices as soon as possible.

The elections to the Azerbaijani Majlis were completed early in December, upon which the council of ministers was formed under Pishevari. The story of the Tabriz autonomous government presents in microcosm the rise and fall of a Communist regime allied with nationalism, with its typical lights and shadows.

The general perception was that, in terms of the improvement of superstructure—paving roads, opening schools and hospitals—Azerbaijan had achieved more in one year under the Democrats than in two decades under the Pahlavi dynasty. The population gladly accepted measures dealing with day-to-day conditions of life, such as price controls, unemployment relief, severe punishment for bribe-taking, and distribution of absentee landlords' properties.

There followed attempts at a veritable cultural revolution aimed at reversing the Pahlavi assimilationist policies. Azeri was decreed the official **language,** and it was introduced to schools at all levels. Textbooks were hastily printed from transliterated versions of **Baku** Cyrillic editions. The process of native cultural revival was highlighted by such events as the opening of the Azerbaijani School of Fine Arts and Painting, the State Theater, the Azerbaijani Broadcasting Agency, and the State University. The revival was carried on with the assistance of Soviet advisers and specialists, to the extent that the language of the fledgling newspapers became infested with Russian-sounding terms. Likewise, the Azerbaijani army that was created, despite the protestations of loyalty to Iran, was Soviet-trained and supplied.

For all the reforms launched by the DPAz government, popular discontent with the regime grew. The clergy were antagonized by the anti-Islamic bias of the DPAz's propaganda, the landowning and wealthy classes became fearful of the possibility of an all-out land reform, and conscription and grain requisitions alienated the peasantry. Meanwhile, Iran appealed to the United Nations for help in securing a Soviet withdrawal from the region. Under pressure from the UN, the Soviet forces left Azerbaijan in May 1946. In November 1946, Iranian troops entered Tabriz to the welcome of the population and put an end to the Autonomous Government of Azerbaijan. *See also* DEMOCRATIC PARTY OF AZERBAIJAN (DPAz, 1945–1960); IRANIAN AZERBAIJAN; MUHAJIRIN (IMMIGRANTS); PISHEVARI, JAFAR SAYYID.

AZADISTAN (LAND OF FREEDOM). The name given to Iran's province of Azerbaijan by the autonomist-regional regime of the **Democratic Party of Azerbaijan** (DPAz) under Shaikh Muhammad **Khiabani** following the April 1920 revolt against the central government of Iran. The leaders of the DPAz chose the name "Azadistan" to emphasize the distinction between it and the independent republic of Azerbaijan under the **Baku** regime, and partly to serve as a model of freedom and independence for the rest of Iran.

The government of Azadistan was formally created in **Tabriz** on June 24, 1920, when Khiabani symbolically moved his office to Ali Kapu, the residence of the viceroy of Azerbaijan. His cabinet included members of the merchant class and some intellectuals. The key positions were held by Khiabani, who was also in charge of finances; Abdul Qasim Fuyuzat, education; Muhammad Savfat, administration of *waqfs* (pious foundations); Muzzafar A'lam Sardat, defense. The DPAz called for the elimination of the foreign presence in Iran, expulsion from **Iranian Azerbaijan** of the officials appointed by the Teheran government, faithful implementation of the constitution, and local autonomy. Although originally a supporter of Soviet Russia, Khiabani became increasingly suspicious of the Bolsheviks, particularly following the establishment of a Russian base of operations at the port of Enzeli where the Bolsheviks could support the Soviet-style regime of Mirza Kuchuk Khan in Gīlān. Following this, the Azadistan regime became an opponent of Soviet Russia, and Azadistan became a sanctuary for enemies of Soviet power from north of the **Araxes River.** The autonomous government of Azadistan was overthrown on September 4, 1920, following the capture of **Tabriz** by Iranian Cossacks sent by the central government of Iran. *See also* DEMOCRATIC PARTY OF AZERBAIJAN (DPAz, 1917–1920); IRANIAN AZERBAIJAN; KHIABANI, SHAIKH MUHAMMAD.

AZARIJILAR (Partisans of Azerbaijan). The supporters of the use of Azeri as the literary **language** of Azerbaijan. They were opposed to the trend toward linguistic Ottomanization. The public debate between the Azarijilar and Ottomanizers was inaugurated in 1903 by the newspaper *Sharq-i Rus* (The Russian East) in an article, "We Lack a Literary Language," by Mammad Agha **Shahtakhtinski.** The controversy grew particularly intense after the 1905 Russian Revolution, and reflected the issue of an emerging Azerbaijani national identity, which was based more on language than on territory. The Azarijilar represented a populist rather than an elitist disposition, and their best-known press organ was the satirical-literary journal *Molla Nasr al-din,* which reveled in describing comic effects produced in Azeri by Ottoman grammar and expressions. An article in the *Molla Nasr al-din,* "The Native Language," by Faridun Kocharli, was more assertive in tone, calling the attempts at Ottomanization equal to national treason. *See also* ALPHABET REFORM; EDUCATION; LANGUAGE, AZERI.

AZERBAIJAN CHEKA (AzCheka). The Azerbaijan Cheka was an offshoot of the Russian Cheka (Extraordinary Commission for Fighting Counterrevolution and Sabotage), which acted as the Bolsheviks' secret police force. It was established on April 29, 1920, immediately after the overthrow of the **Azerbaijani Democratic Republic.** Although officially independent, the AzCheka was controlled by the Central Committee of the Russian Communist Party. The head of the AzCheka was Mir Jafar Abbasovich Baghirov, who would later rise to become first secretary of the **Communist Party of Azerbaijan** in the 1930s. One of the AzCheka's early recruits was Lavrentii P. Beria who would later become head of the Soviet NKVD. Beria served under Baghirov from February 1921 to November 1922. The AzCheka carried out operations against the Bolsheviks' political enemies such as the Right-Musavatists, Pan-Islamists, and Socialist Revolutionaries. It had the power of summary execution over suspects and was responsible for much of the bloodshed that secured Bolshevik power in Azerbaijan. The AzCheka was replaced in 1926 by the Azerbaijani OGPU. (political police). *See also* BAGHIROV, MIR JAFAR.

AZERBAIJAN STATE PETROLEUM ACADEMY. Founded in 1920 as the Baku Polytechnical Institute, it trains engineers in oil extraction, oil refining, and the petrochemical industry. The graduates of this school form the bulk of Azerbaijan's technocratic elite, and they took part in developing the oil industry in various regions of the USSR as well as in the countries of the Middle East, Africa, and Asia. The institute's name has undergone several alterations throughout its existence: the Azerbaijan Polytechnical Institute (1928–1930), the Petroleum Institute (1930–1934), the Industrial Institute (1934–1959), the Azerbaijan Institute of Petroleum and Chemistry (1959–1990), and finally its present name. The institute has seven departments: geologic prospecting, oil extraction, chemistry and technology, petroleum industry machines, power engineering, production process automation, and engineering and economics. It contains a graduate school, research laboratories, and libraries. The institute confers advanced degrees in geology, mineralogy, technical sciences, and chemistry. *See also* OIL INDUSTRY.

AZERBAIJANI DEMOCRATIC REPUBLIC (1918–1920). The first independent Azerbaijani nation-state was proclaimed on May 28, 1918, by the **Azerbaijani National Council** consisting of the Muslim members of the legislature of the just dissolved **Transcaucasian Federation.** The full name of the new state was Azerbaijan Democratic (*Khalq*) Republic. **Ganja** was designated as its temporary capital and Fath Ali Khan **Khoiski** was appointed the head of government.

Shortly after its declaration of independence, Azerbaijan signed a treaty of friendship with Ottoman Turkey. The treaty guaranteed Ottoman assistance to the new nation, but did not recognize Azerbaijan's independent statehood since the Turks still expected to include Azerbaijan in the Ottoman Empire. Nuri Pasha, the commander of the **Army of Islam** objected to the composition of the Khoiski cabinet on the grounds that it included leftist elements as well as those inclined toward Azerbaijani nationalism. On June 17, Khan Khoiski formed his second cabinet, acceptable to Nuri. At the same time, the National Council fulfilled another of Nuri's wishes by transferring its powers to the Council of Ministers, pending the convocation of the Azerbaijani Constituent Assembly. There followed other measures associated with the Ottoman pressure: land reform was suspended, the labor unions were suppressed, and socialist activities were banned. In general, the policies under the Ottoman military rule were perceived as eroding the achievements of the Russian Revolution, and their ultimate aim was seen as *Ilhaq,* some form of unification with the Ottoman state.

With the entry of Ottoman forces into **Baku** on September 16, 1918, the Azerbaijan government moved to the nation's capital. Following Turkey's surrender in October 1918, the Ottoman army evacuated Azerbaijan, and Baku was occupied by British troops under Major-General W. M. Thomson. The British kept garrisons in some towns, notably in Baku, where they proclaimed martial law. They controlled railways, especially the Baku–Batum line over which oil exports again began to flow. Their involvement extended into some branches of civilian administration—the currency issue, food supply, and mediation of labor disputes in the oil fields and railways. On the other hand, unlike the Ottomans, they refrained from interfering in the politics of the Azerbaijani state.

The Azerbaijani elite showed its political acumen by playing to the democratic sensitivities of the British. On the eve of Thomson's landing in Baku, the National Council reconvened from its Ottoman-imposed hibernation. Assuming, significantly, the name "Parliament," the body enlarged itself by co-opting new members and representatives of national minorities.

The Parliament consisted of 120 deputies, 96 of whom joined by the time of its inauguration on December 7, 1918. The **Musavat** was represented by 38 deputies; the **Ittihad** by 13; the Socialists, including the **Muslim Socialist Bloc,** and the Menshevik **Himmat** by 13; the Ahrar (Liberal) Party by 5; Independents by 5; the **Dashnaktsutiun** (Armenian Revolutionary Federation) by 6; other Armenians by 5; and other national minorities by 5.

With such a distribution of mandates, coalition cabinets that dissolved in governmental crises became a feature of Azerbaijani politics. There were five cabinets in two years of independence. All but the last were put together without ministers from the Ittihad, the party that acquired the status of quasi-permanent opposition. The first three cabinets were headed by Khan Khoiski, the other two by Nasib bey **Yusufbeyli** (Ussubekov). The instability of the executive enhanced the importance of the Parliament, which became the focus of Azerbaijani political life. The office of the president of the Parliament, held by Ali Mardan bey **Topchibashi,** was recognized as the head of state.

The withdrawal of the British troops, completed in August 1919, ushered in the phase of full independence. Ironically, the absence of an outside power's tutelage marked the twilight of the Democratic Republic. As the Russian Red Army pushed south in pursuit of the Whites, there were no grounds for assuming that the Reds would stop at Azerbaijan's frontier, and against this peril Baku sought frantically for assurances. A back door attempt to return to British protection was made through negotiating a confederative link to Iran, but the maneuver fell through when the Iranian Majlis refused to ratify the Anglo-Iranian Agreement of 1919.

In March 1920, as the 11th Red Army began to occupy neighboring **Daghestan,** dissension had come into the open within the Baku ruling coalition. Likewise, the rift in the ranks of the **Musavat** between the right and left wings reemerged more sharply than ever before. The spokesman for the Left, Interior Minister Mammad Hasan **Hajinski,** urged a "placate Russia" policy against the tougher-minded foreign minister, Khan Khoiski. Meanwhile, an Armenian uprising broke out in **Nagorno-Karabagh** on March 23, and the Azerbaijani high command committed most of the army against the insurgents, denuding its frontier with Russia. On April 1, the cabinet of Yusufbeyli resigned, and Hajinski began his attempts to form a government with participation of the Communists. After three weeks of negotiations, the Communists declined and began preparations for a coup set for April 27. Before their weak fighting squads began action, the Red Army's armored trains had crossed the frontier heading for Baku. Here, the Azerbaijani Revolutionary Committee (**Azrevkom**) handed an ultimatum to the Parliament demanding the surrender of its powers. With the acceptance of the ultimatum, the independent Azerbaijani state ended its existence on April 28, 1920. *See also* ARMY OF ISLAM; AZERBAIJANI NATIONAL COUNCIL; MUSAVAT.

AZERBAIJANI NATIONAL COUNCIL. The legislative body formed by the Azerbaijani parliamentary group of the **Transcaucasian Seim** which, upon the dissolution of the **Transcaucasian Federation,** proclaimed Azerbaijan an independent state on May 28, 1918. The Council chose Fath Ali Khan **Khoiski** as the prime minister, and designated **Ganja** as the interim capital of the new republic.

The National Council began its work amidst friction with the Ottoman occupation authorities. The commander of the **Army of Islam,** Nuri Pasha, let it be known that his sympathies lay with conservatives and Pan-Islamic or Pan-Turanian elements rather than with the Leftists or Musavatists, who might be suspected of being in an "Azerbaijan first" frame of mind. He did not show much regard for the National Council, as this body owed its existence to the Russian Revolution.

In protest against Ottoman meddling, the deputies of **Himmat** and the Socialist Bloc withdrew from the Council, and on June 17 a compromise went into effect. Khan Khoiski presented his second cabinet, which included six new members. The same day, the National Council transferred its prerogatives to the new government of Azerbaijan, which thereupon assumed legislative powers pending the convocation of the Azerbaijani Constituent Assembly. In mid-November 1918, on the eve of the arrival of British occupation forces in **Baku,** the Council reconvened and, after co-opting representatives of national minorities and additional deputies of political parties, constituted itself into the Parliament. *See also* TRANSCAUCASIAN FEDERATION; TRANSCAUCASIAN SEIM.

AZERBAIJANI REPUBLIC. *See* REPUBLIC OF AZERBAIJAN.

AZERBAIJANI SOVIET SOCIALIST REPUBLIC (AZERBAIJANI SSR). Created under the Stalin Constitution of 1936 in which Azerbaijan became a constituent republic of the USSR. The same status was bestowed on Armenia and Georgia, the two other members of the **Transcaucasian Soviet Federated Socialist Republic** (TSFSR), which had been in existence since March 12, 1922. The TSFSR was dissolved, presumably to prevent formation of regional blocs, and only vertical links with Moscow, instead of horizontal with other republics, were allowed.

The Azerbaijani SSR's constitution echoed the Stalin Constitution of the USSR in that it affirmed a commitment to Marxism-Leninism, the construction of socialism, and the equality of citizens and nationalities. The republic was declared a Soviet state of workers and peasants where a socialist system of economy and property existed. Azerbaijan was now a full-fledged member of the USSR, equal with all other union republics. Its right to secede was affirmed, and no changes to its territory were legal without the republic's approval. The authority of the republic over the **Nakhichevan Autonomous Soviet Socialist Republic** and the **Nagorno-Karabagh** district were confirmed. The Azerbaijani SSR remained in existence until the dissolution of the USSR in 1991, when the independent **Republic of Azerbaijan** was proclaimed in its place. *See also* REPUBLIC OF AZERBAIJAN; NAGORNO-KARABAGH; TRANSCAUCASIAN SOVIET FEDERATED SOCIALIST REPUBLIC.

AZERI PEOPLE. Throughout their history, the people of Azerbaijan have been referred to as Azerbaijanians, Azeris, Azeri Turks, Azeri Tatars, Tatars of Transcaucasia, Caucasian Tatars, Turks, and Tiurks. They are a Turkic-speaking people living in the **Azerbaijani Republic** and northwest Iran (**Iranian Azerbaijan**). A considerable number also live in the Iranian cities of Teheran and Qum, and in the Iranian province of Khorāsān. There are an estimated 15 million Azeris in Iran, and more than 7 million in the Azerbaijani Republic. Although the Azeris speak a Turkic language they are of mixed Turkic, Iranian, and Caucasian ethnic background. They are predominantly Shi'ite Muslim in religion, with a significant Sunni Muslim minority, especially north of the **Araxes River** border. Among the Iranian Azeris there are three smaller seminomadic groups that maintain distinct identities: the Airum, Padar, and Shahseven.

The following statistics are for the Azerbaijani Republic only:
Births (per 1,000 pop.) = 22
Infant mortality (per 1,000 live births 1997) = 74
Average life expectancy at birth (1997) = 60.3 male; 69.9 female
Urban population = 56%
Population density = 232 per sq. mi.

AZIZBEKOV, MESHADI AZIZBEYOGHLI (1870–1918). An engineer who became a professional revolutionary and a leading member of the **Himmat Party**. As a member of the Russian Social-Democratic Workers Party, Azizbekov joined the Himmat in early 1905, strengthening its leadership in the face of the challenges of the Russian Revolution. In 1918 he became one of the leaders of the **Baku Commune,**

and was made its commissar for the Baku guberniia with a special mission of enlisting the support of the Muslim rural masses. Following the collapse of the Baku Commune, Azizbekov was among the 26 **Baku commissars** who were shot on September 20, 1918, by social revolutionaries outside Krasnovodsk, across the Caspian Sea. *See also* HIMMAT; BAKU COMMUNE.

AZREVKOM (AZERBAIJANI REVOLUTIONARY COMMIT-TEE). A native Azerbaijani Bolshevik group in charge of carrying out the overthrow of the government of the **Azerbaijani Democratic Republic.** Azrevkom was headed by Nariman N. **Narimanov** and its members were Mirza Davud **Huseynov,** H. M. Musabekov, Dadash H. Buniatzade, A. Alimov, and Ali Haidar Karayev. On the eve of the Red Army's invasion (April 27, 1920) the Azrevkom declared the government of the Azerbaijani Democratic Republic "treacherous, criminal, counterrevolutionary," and proclaimed Azerbaijan a Soviet Socialist Republic. Then it appealed to Soviet Russia for military assistance. On April 28, 1920, the Azrevkom formed the Soviet of People's Commissars under the chairmanship of Nariman N. Narimanov to act as a provisional government. The Bolshevik takeover was completed on April 30, 1920, as advance units of the 11th Red Army occupied **Baku** and its environs. *See also* COMMUNIST PARTY OF AZERBAIJAN.

-B-

BABAK (798–838). The leader of a popular uprising against Arab rule in Azerbaijan and western Iran from 816 to 837. Babak was born in southern Azerbaijan and was the son of a petty tradesman. As a youth he was a shepherd, camel driver, and apprentice to a craftsman in **Tabriz.** He became an adherent of the **Khurramiya** sect. After his assumption of the leadership of the Khurramiya in 816, he launched a revolt against the Abbasid Caliph Ma'mun (813–833), which became known as the **Babak Uprising.** Following the failure of the revolt he was captured by the forces of the Caliph and executed. *See also* BABAK UPRISING.

BABAK UPRISING (816–837). The Babak Uprising raged for 21 years in Azerbaijan and western Iran. It was started and headed by the leader of the **Khurramiya** sect, **Babak.** Although the adherents of the Khurramiya, were mostly peasants and artisans, the uprising was soon joined by landowners who resented Arab control. The forces of the Abbasid Caliph Ma'mun (813–833) were expelled from almost all of Azerbaijan, some provinces of Iran, and eastern Armenia by the rebels, who numbered about 300,000.

The Abbasid caliphate was unable to effectively combat the rebels due to its preoccupation with a war against the Byzantine Empire, and an additional uprising in Egypt. However, after concluding a peace treaty with the Byzantine emperor in 833, Caliph Mutasim (833–842) brought the bulk of his forces to bear against the rebellion. The rebels were seriously weakened after suffering a severe defeat near Hamadān in 833, losing, according to Arab sources, 60,000 men. Resistance was crushed after the Caliph's greatest general, Haidar ibn-Kaus, was placed in command of the caliph's armies. The remnants of the rebel army retreated to the fortress of Badz. Following a protracted siege, the fortress was taken in 837, and all resistance was crushed. *See also* BABAK.

BABISM. A Shi'ite religious-social movement which flourished in **Iranian Azerbaijan** during the 1840s. It was founded by Sayyid **Ali Muhammad,** the merchant-saint who proclaimed himself the *Bab* (gateway) to the Hidden Imam. He called for the defense of freedom, the safeguarding of private property against government taxation and confiscation, and the rights of the provinces to self-government. The movement appealed to the restive and economically suffering middle classes. In 1848 Babism officially seceded from Islam, and its growing militancy led to the Zanjān revolt in 1850. Babism was crushed by the forces of Shah Nasr ul-Din following Sayyid Ali Muhammad's execution in 1852. *See also* ALI MUHAMMAD, SAYYID.

BAGHIROV, KAMRAN M. First secretary of the **Communist Party of Azerbaijan** from 1982 to 1988. Baghirov succeeded Haidar **Aliyev** as first secretary upon his promotion to higher office in 1982. Under his leadership open corruption and economic mismanagement combined to destabilize the country. His mishandling of the **Nagorno-Karabagh** crisis probably contributed to his removal from office in May 1988, although the official explanation was ill health. His successor as first secretary of the Communist Party of Azerbaijan was **Abdul Rakhman Vazirov.** *See also* COMMUNIST PARTY OF AZERBAIJAN.

BAGHIROV, MIR JAFAR ABBASOVICH (1896–1956). Commissar for internal affairs from 1921 to 1933 and the head of the **Communist Party of Azerbaijan** from 1933 to 1953. His political career was closely linked to that of Lavrentii P. Beria, the interior commissar of the USSR. As the head of the CPAz, Baghirov carried out Stalin's policies within Azerbaijan. By 1940 an estimated 70,000 Azeris had died as a result of purges carried out under Baghirov. The **intelligentsia** was decimated, broken, and eliminated as a social force. Likewise, the old guard Communist elite was destroyed. During **World War II** he promoted close ties between Soviet and **Iranian Azerbaijan.** Following Beria's downfall after the death of Stalin in 1953, Baghirov was removed from office. In 1956 he was tried, sentenced to death for crimes against the state, and executed. His trial marked the official beginning of the de-Stalinization campaign in Azerbaijan. Baghirov's successor was Imam Dashdemiroghlu **Mustafayev.** *See also* COMMUNIST PARTY OF AZERBAIJAN; IRANIAN AZERBAIJAN.

BAKIKHANOV (BAKIKHANLI), ABBAS QULU AGHA (1794–1847). Azerbaijani writer and scholar, who, despite his traditional Islamic education, became a precursor of the native enlightenment movement. Exposed to European influences through his service in the Russian administration and the army, he proposed the reform of primary schools as the means to improved social conditions. Among his writings is the comprehensive history of Azerbaijan, *Gulistan-i Iram* (The Flower Garden). A thinker with encyclopedic interest, he wrote also on pedagogy and philosophy, phonetics and morphology, morals and manners, astronomy and geography, as well as purely literary works of poetry and prose. *See also* LITERATURE.

BAKU. The capital and largest city of Azerbaijan. The name "Baku" is possibly a contraction of the Iranian words *bad khube* (bad winds). The city is located on the western coast of the **Caspian Sea** on the south shore of the **Apsheron Peninsula.** The metropolitan area of Greater Baku, 1,360 square miles (2,192 sq km), occupies a considerable part of the peninsula.

By the 11th century, Baku was in the possession of the **Shirvanshahs** who made it their capital in the second half of the 12th century. For a period in the 13th and 14th centuries it came under the sway of the Mongols. After a protracted siege, Baku was seized by the forces of **Safavid** Iran in 1540. In the 1580s the Ottoman Empire captured Baku and held it until 1604 when the town was recaptured by the troops of **Shah Abbas I.** In 1723 Baku was taken by the troops of Peter the Great, but was returned to Iran in 1735. In 1747 the town became the capital of the **Baku Khanate** and survived in this quasi-independent status until annexation by Russia in 1806.

With the development of the **oil industry** in the 1870s Baku became the fastest-growing urban center in the Russian Empire. The city experienced an influx of **Armenians** and Russians attracted by high-paying industrial and administrative positions. Immigrants from the countryside as well as from **Iranian Azerbaijan** found employment as unskilled laborers in the oil fields. Jointly, the Muslim population usually accounted for less than half of the inhabitants in the late 19th and early 20th century.

Baku and its environs were the scene of intercommunal violence between Azeris and Armenians in 1905–1906 and again in 1918. Following the massacre of the **Azeris,** known as the **March Days,** the Soviet-type of government known as the **Baku Commune** was established on April 25, 1918, and remained in existence for the next three months. In September 1918, upon the entry of the Ottoman forces, Baku became the capital of the **Azerbaijani Democratic Republic** from September 15, 1918, until its overthrow on April 28, 1920.

During the Soviet period, Baku experienced further urban growth. The Caspian oil fueled the Soviet Union's war effort during **World War II,** and the oil fields were the objective of the great, but unsuccessful, German offensive in 1942 In the post-war period, however, Baku oil lost its relative weight in the Soviet Union's economy, and the industry began to decline. In step with the economic trend, the city's population began to change its multiethnic character with the slow but steady out-migration of Armenian and Russian inhabitants.

The current population of Baku is 1,757,000. Approximately one-fourth of the inhabitants of Azerbaijan, and nearly half of its urban population, is concentrated in Baku. The Baku oil industry, reviving in the post-Soviet period with Western investments, is again a base for the city's economy. Other, more labor intensive industries include production of oil extraction and processing equipment, shipbuilding and repair, manufacture of electrical machinery, chemicals, cement, textiles, footwear, and foodstuffs.

The city is also the main center of Azerbaijani cultural and educational life with several universities and other institutions of higher learning, theaters, museums, art galleries, and research institutes.

Baku is a major port on the **Caspian Sea.** It acquired this importance in the 19th century with the expansion of trade between Russia and Iran. The development of the region's oil industry in the 1870s and 1880s together with the construction of a railroad linking the city with Tbilisi, Batumi, and the general Russian rail network, promoted its rapid growth. Between 1929 and 1937 the Soviets rebuilt and modernized the port facilities to handle the increased freight turnover. The port became an important transportation junction linking Baku with Astrakhan, the oil bases of the Volga basin, Central Asia, and Iran. *See also* BAKU COMMUNE; OIL INDUSTRY.

BAKU COMMISSARS. Twenty-six Bolshevik leaders of the **Baku Commune,** shot near Krasnovodsk on September 20, 1918. After the fall of **Baku** into Ottoman hands, they were arrested by the British-supported Krasnovodsk social revolutionaries, having fled the city to the eastern coast of the **Caspian Sea.** Among the prisoners were Stepan G. **Shaumian,** chairman of the Baku Council of People's Commissars (Sovnarkom), Meshadi A. **Azizbekov,** provincial commissar of the Sovnarkom, Prokofii A. Dzhaparidze, commissar of internal affairs, I. T. Fioletov, commissar for the economy, and M. G. Vazirov, commissar for agriculture. Except for the latter and Azizbekov, all of the commissars were non-Azeris.

Their execution became the most publicized case of martyrdom for the cause of the Bolshevik revolution. Their remains were buried in the town square of Baku, which was renamed the Square of the Twenty-Six Baku Commissars. The monument that was raised over their grave at the time was destroyed following the 1991 declaration of independence. *See also* BAKU COMMUNE.

BAKU COMMUNE. A Soviet-type government formed in **Baku** and its environs on April 25, 1918, following the outbreak of ethnic violence in Baku known as the **March Days.** The term "commune" harked back to the example of Paris in 1871, and connoted the dictatorship of the proletariat on a local scale but in union with the whole of Russia. A series of radical reforms was hastily enacted under the aegis of the Commune by its executive body, the Baku Sovnarkom, whose head was the Armenian Bolshevik Stepan **Shaumian.** These reforms included reorganization of courts and the schools, as well as expropriation of banks, shipping companies, fisheries, and the **oil industry.** For all of its zeal, the Baku Sovnarkom showed a degree of moderation toward its political opponents. The reason was the inherently weak political position of the Bolsheviks in the city. A minority within the city soviet, they were supported only by Russian Left social revolutionaries (SRs), and acquiesced to by Right SRs, Mensheviks, and Dashnakists. Moreover, the makeup of the Baku Soviet was not representative of the largest segment of the population, the Muslims whom, in the words of Soviet historian Ia. Ratgauzer, the Bolsheviks regarded as, "immature from the revolutionary standpoint and culturally inferior." Bolshevik relations with the Muslims were rendered more difficult by the fact that the Dashnakists wielded powerful influence in the Baku Soviet, and even more in its armed forces, which were 70 percent Armenian and under the command of an Armenian officer, Colonel Z. Avetisian. When the Baku Red Army made a risky and abortive attempt at an offensive at **Ganja,** the Armenian soldiers let loose their hostility toward the Muslim population in incidents of looting and violence. The defeat of the Red forces at Geokchai, and the subsequent counteroffensive of the **Army of Islam,** brought to a head the simmering political crisis in Baku, a city ill-prepared for defense. Those who were neither Bolsheviks nor Muslims began to agitate openly for inviting the British Expeditionary Force of Major-General Lionel **Dunsterville,** stationed in the Iranian port of Enzeli. On July 25, the broadened Baku Soviet, its majority made up of Dashnakists, Right Social Revolutionaries, and Mensheviks, voted to call for the help of the British. The Baku Sovnarkom resigned in protest, and on July 26, the Commune, after 97 days of existence, was succeeded by the **Central Caspian Dictatorship.** In the eyes of the **Azeris,** the Commune was another example of Bolshevik–Armenian collusion. *See also* BAKU COMMISSARS.

BAKU KHANATE. An Azerbaijani principality that was centered around the town of **Baku.** Arising in 1747, after the assassination of Iran's ruler **Nadir Shah,** its economy was based on agriculture, salt, and oil extraction, as well as on the transit trade. The Baku Khanate was occupied by Russian troops in 1806 during the first **Russo-Iranian War (1804–1813).** Russian conquest of the khanate was ratified by the Treaty of **Gulistan** (1813) in which Iran renounced its sovereignty over a large part of northern Azerbaijan. Russia's rule was further acknowledged by the Treaty of **Turkmanchai** (1828) following the second **Russo-Iranian War (1826–1828).** After the Turkmanchai settlement the Baku Khanate was abolished and the area became a part of the Russian Empire.

BAKU STATE UNIVERSITY. Opened under the **Azerbaijani Democratic Republic** in September 1919, this first institution of higher learning in Azerbaijan was transferred from Tbilisi, where it had been conceived as the University of **Transcaucasia.** Its founder was the Russian scientist V. I. Razumovskii. The language of instruction was Russian, and initially the university consisted of two departments, medical and historical-philological.

Under the Soviet *korenizatsiia* (nativization) policy of the 1920s the university was gradually Turkified, and by the end of the decade 70 percent of the students and 75 percent of the faculty were **Azeris.** The university ceased to exist in 1930 after it was reorganized into several independent educational institutions, and the nativization policy began to be replaced by Russification. The university was restored four years later and renamed after Sergei M. Kirov, but it suffered heavy losses during Stalin's purges of the 1930s, with at least 30 faculty members losing their lives.

Toward the end of the Soviet period, the university included 12 departments, as well as an astronomical station, computer center, library, and museum. In 1990, its name was changed again, this time to the University of Mammad Amin **Rasulzade.**

BIRIYA, MUHAMMAD (1914–1985). A prominent figure in far left politics as well as in the literature of **Iranian Azerbaijan.** Following the entry of the Red Army into northern Iran in 1941, Biriya became one of the founders of the leftist Iranian Tudeh Party, and a leading member of its **Tabriz** chapter. He was also active as a labor organizer. Upon the creation of the **Democratic Party of Azerbaijan** in the fall of 1945, he brought into its ranks the Tabriz Worker's Union. In the party leadership his special responsibilities were education and culture. Biriya was a driving spirit behind the establishment of the Azerbaijani State Theater, the School of Fine Arts, the State University, and the Broadcasting Agency. He oversaw introduction of Azeri as the **language** of instruction in all schools. An ardent proponent of close ties with Soviet Azerbaijan, he headed the Society of Friends of the USSR. In the last days of the **Autonomous Government of Azerbaijan,** Biriya was in favor of resisting the arrival of central government forces. Reports had it that he had been killed by an angry mob when the regime collapsed. In fact, Biriya succeeded in escaping into Soviet Azerbaijan, only to become a victim of the purge of the Democrats after **Pishevari**'s death. Of his 33 years in exile in the USSR, Biriya spent 22 in Soviet jails. Following the overthrow of the monarchy in Iran, he returned to Tabriz, where soon after he was arrested and died in an Iranian prison. Among the lasting achievements of his life are his collections of Azeri poetry. He is recognized as one of the most gifted Azeri poets of the 20th century. *See also* AUTONOMOUS GOVERNMENT OF AZERBAIJAN; DEMOCRATIC PARTY OF AZERBAIJAN; IRANIAN AZERBAIJAN.

BIRLIK (UNION). A socialist Muslim workers association of Volga Tatars in Azerbaijan from 1918 to 1919. Birlik was affiliated with the **Himmat Party**, and remained under its political guidance.

BLACK JANUARY 1990. Following continued tensions over **Nagorno-Karabagh,** on January 13 and 14, 1990, ethnic clashes broke out in **Baku** with an attack by crowds of **Azeris** on residences of **Armenians.** Thirty-two Armenians and an unknown number of Azeris were killed. Many more were wounded. The government security forces remained remarkably absent or passive during the riots. After the disturbances had run their course by January 15, the Presidium of the USSR Supreme Soviet ordered 11,000 army and KGB troops under the command of General Alexander Lebed to Azerbaijan and Armenia. Although Moscow announced that the troops were only there to restore order, it soon became apparent that the real purpose was to prevent the takeover of power by the **People's Front of Azerbaijan** (PFAz). On January 16 barricades began to go up on the roads entering Baku. By January 20 Soviet troops occupied the city, using extreme force to subdue the population. The number of civilians killed was reliably established at 168, the wounded at 715, and more than 400 persons remained unaccounted for. PFAz leaders were arrested, its offices closed, and files seized. Abrupt changes also followed within the **Communist Party of Azerbaijan** (CPAz) leadership: First Secretary Abdurrahman **Vazirov** was replaced by Ayaz Niyazi **Mutalibov.**

Public opinion in Azerbaijan turned solidly against the CPAz and thousands publicly burned their party cards. A resolution of the Supreme Soviet of Azerbaijan demanded the withrawal of the troops and lifting of the Moscow-imposed state of emergency, threatening "discussion on the question of maintaining Azerbaijan's relationship with the USSR." The main effect of the Soviet military intervention was to strengthen the nationalist sentiment among the population. *See also* NAGORNO-KARABAGH DISPUTE.

-C-

CASPIAN CONTROVERSY. A legal and politcal dispute centered on the question: is the Caspian a sea or a lake? The treaties concluded between Russia and Iran in 1921 and 1940, stipulated the joint use of the Caspian, inaccessible to other countries. With the breakup of the Soviet Union there are five independent states on the Caspian littoral— Azerbaijan, Kazakhstan, and Turkmenistan, in addition to Russia and Iran. In 1993–94 the Russian foreign ministry insisted on a joint exploitation as well as protection of all Caspian resources, a position supported by Iran. The evolution of the dispute has shown that Moscow is divided on the Caspian issue and that pragmatic business groups had increasing leverage in shaping policy toward the region at variance with the foreign ministry. The Lukoil company was instrumental in Russia's de facto acceptance of the division of the Caspain seabed into national sectors. *See also* OIL INDUSTRY.

CASPIAN SEA. The sea's name is derived from the Greek *Kaspion pelagos*. It is the world's largest inland body of water, bordered by the countries of Kazakhstan, Turkmenistan, Azerbaijan, Iran, and Russia. It receives its name from the **Caspians**, a tribe that inhabited its eastern shores. It has also been called the Hyrcanian, Khvalyn (Khvaliss), and Khazar Seas (the latter is the Azeri and Turkish name).

The Caspian Sea extends 744 miles (1,200 km) from north to south, and is 270 miles (434 km) wide. Its shoreline is 4,375 miles long, and its area is 143,550 square miles (371,795 sq km). It is 94 feet (28.5 m) below sea level; the maximum depth is 3,363 feet (1,025 m). More than 130 rivers flow into the Caspian Sea, with Volga supplying about 80 percent of the inflowing water. The sea is an important part of Azerbaijan's **economy** with its many varieties of fish, including sturgeon and their caviar. It is a substantial source of offshore oil, producing most of Azerbaijan's oil revenue. Also of economic importance is the mining of sodium sulfate, mirabilite, and epsomite. In addition, the sea serves the needs of passenger and commercial transportation.

The heavy industry and large population of the Caspian region have severely affected the ecology of the sea. Its waters have been heavily polluted, especially in the vicinity of the metropolitan area of Baku and the chemical industry center of Sumgait, by the dumping of organic and industrial wastes. *See also* OIL INDUSTRY.

CASPIANS. First mentioned by Herodotus in the fifth century B.C., the Caspians were nomadic tribes of the Ibero-Caucasian group who raised livestock along the steppe regions of eastern Azerbaijan. Sometime before the first century B.C. they merged with the Medes, Albani, and other tribes. Their name was applied to the **Caspian Sea** and also to its coastal region.

CAUCASIA. A region between the Black Sea, the Sea of Azov, and the **Caspian Sea,** stretching from the Kuma-Manych depression in the north to the Turkish and Iranian borders in the south. It comprises 170,000 square miles (440,000 sq km) and is divided into the Northern Caucasus and **Transcaucasia.** The Northern Caucasus belongs to the Russian Federation and Transcaucasia is divided between Azerbaijan, Armenia, and Georgia.

CAUCASIAN ALBANIA. A kingdom in northern Azerbaijan in the first century B.C. Its capital was the city of Kabala (Kabalaka). It also encompassed the territory around **Shirvan** and **Daghestan.** The kingdom of Albania was allied with Georgia and Armenia against the campaigns of the Roman general Lucullus (69–67 B.C.) and against Pompey during his campaign against Mithradates the Great (66–65 B.C.). During the reign of Emperor Hadrian their territory was invaded by the Alani. Christianity became the state religion in the early fourth century A.D. During the third and fourth centuries Albania became a vassal of Sassanid Persia. In 450–451 it was involved in the revolt of the Armenian prince Vardan Mamikonian against the Sassanids. The ruling Albanian dynasty was destroyed in the sixth century by the Sassanids. Albania regained its independence briefly, but was conquered by the Arabs in the seventh century. Following the Arab conquest many Albanians converted to Islam. Although Albanian princes managed to gain independence for short periods of time during the period of Arab rule, the country eventually disappeared as a separate entity, and the remaining Albanian people were driven into Armenia by the Khazars.

CAUCASIAN COMMITTEE. A body established in 1845 by the Russian imperial government in connection with the introduction of the all-Russian administrative system into the region of the Caucasus.

It consisted of the ministers of war, finance, state properties, justice, and internal affairs, as well as the heir to the throne, the head of the police, and other high officials appointed by the tsar. The Caucasian Committee directed the civilian activity of the imperial administration in the Caucasus. The Committee was abolished in 1882 after the full integration of the Caucasus with the new administrative system of the Russian state.

CAUCASUS MOUNTAINS. A mountain range that separates Europe from Asia. It extends from the Black Sea to the **Caspian Sea,** and divides the area of Caucasia into the Northern Caucasus and **Transcaucasia.** The highest ranges along the axial zone of the Greater Caucasus are the Glavnyi and the Bokovoi. The highest peaks are the Dombai-Ul'gen 13,274 feet (4,046 m), Elbrus 18,510 feet (5,642 m), Shkhara 16,627 feet (5,068 m), Dykhtau 17,070 feet (5,203 m), Kazbek 16,512 feet (5,033 m), Tebulosmta 14,741 feet (4,493 m), and Bazardiuziu 14,652 feet (4,466 m). *See also* LOWER CAUCASUS RANGE.

CENTRAL CASPIAN DICTATORSHIP (TSENTROKASPIY). A provisional government set up in **Baku** following the collapse of the **Baku Commune.** It was brought about by the withdrawal from Baku of the force under Cossack colonel Lazar Bicherakhov at the end of July 1918, which left the city virtually defenseless in the face of the advancing Ottoman armies. In response to the threat, the Baku Soviet (the majority of which were Dashnakists, rightist social revolutionaries, and Mensheviks) voted to invite the British to defend the city on July 25. The Baku Sovnarkom, the majority of which were Bolsheviks, resigned en masse in protest of this move. The **Central Caspian Dictatorship** representing the non-Azeri population, succeeded the government of the Baku Commune on July 26. The British force, under Major-General Lionel C. **Dunsterville,** arrived in Baku in mid-August, but could do little to prevent the capture of Baku, which fell to the Ottoman forces on September 15, 1918. On September 20, 1918, members of the Baku Sovnarkom who had fled the city, the **Baku Commissars,** were shot in Krasnovodsk by anti-Bolshevik forces. Following the Ottoman entry into Baku the government of the **Azerbaijani Democratic Republic** transferred its offices to the city. *See also* BAKU COMMISSARS; BAKU COMMUNE.

CHECHENO-INGUSHETIA. An autonomous republic within the Russian Federation, situated on the northern slopes of the great **Caucasus Mountain** range and bordering Stavropol' Kray, Daghestan, Georgia, and Ossetia. The republic covered 7,452 square miles (19,300 sq km), and its population in 1989 was 1,270,000. Of this total, Chechens accounted for 58 percent, Russians for 23 percent, and Ingush for 13 percent.

From the end of the 18th century Chechnya was a center of opposition to Russia's expansion southward. The movement of Shaikh Mansur at the close of the 18th century, the struggle of **Shamil** in the mid-19th century, the emirate of Uzun Haji during the Russian Civil War, were all part of a long tradition of Chechen resistance.

The republic was established in 1936 by combining the autonomous Chechen and Ingush *oblasts*. When the Chechens and Ingush were accused of collaboration with the Germans in **World War II,** the republic was dissolved and its non-Russian inhabitants deported to Central Asia. They were allowed to return in 1957 under Nikita Khrushchev, and the republic was restored. After the breakup of the USSR, Chechnya and Ingush became separate republics within Russia in 1992, and in Chechnya a movement for secession from Russia developed. In December 1994, Russia launched a military attack on Chechnya resulting in one of the most violent and prolonged armed conflicts of the 1990s. The last Russian troops remaining in Chechnya were pulled out in January 1997. *See also* CAUCASIA; SHAMIL.

COMMUNIST PARTY OF AZERBAIJAN (CPAz). Founded on February 13, 1920, in **Baku** through the merger of the local branch of the Russian Communist Party (Bolshevik), the **Himmat Party**, and **Adalat** Party. Its 43-man Central Committee consisted primarily of **Azeris,** with Mirza Davud **Huseynov** as chairman. The Communist Party of Azerbaijan, in conjunction with the Red Army, carried out a coup against the **Azerbaijani Democratic Republic** on April 27, 1920. Following the overthrow of the Republic, the provisional Azerbaijani Revolutionary Committee (**Azrevkom**) was formed under Nariman Narimanov.

The Azrevkom was replaced by the Soviet of People's Commissars (Sovnarkom) at the first All-Azerbaijan Congress of Soviets on May

19, 1921. The composition of the party at this time was only about 43 percent Azeri, with the rest being Russian and **Armenian.** Among the ethnic Azeri leaders an internecine struggle was waged between the old guard symbolized by Narimanov, and the "young" who had joined the Himmat shortly before the end of independence. Other controversies within the party were fueled by the spirit of national communism, whose spokesman in the 1920s, Eyyub Khanbudagov, called for the linguistic assimilation of the nonnative population of **Baku.**

The CPAz presided over such campaigns as **alphabet reform,** emancipation of women, the anti-Islamic drive, collectivization of agriculture, and industrialization. The collectivization campaign, marked by massive brutalities, brought to prominence Mir Jafar **Baghirov,** formerly the head of the Azerbaijani OGPU (political police), who in 1933 became first secretary of the CPAz. After coming to power, he launched a campaign of denunciation against the long-dead Narimanov, calling him "bourgeois nationalist" or "anti-Communist." This sent a message to companions and associates of Narimanov who thus became politically paralyzed before facing even worse fates.

In 1937 and 1938 Stalin's great purges were carried out in Azerbaijan under the supervision of Baghirov. The purge destroyed the majority of the party leadership, "old" and "young" Himmatists alike. Among the prominent victims were such men as Hamid Sultanov, Sultan Efendiyev, Ruhulla Akhundov, Ali Heydar Karayev, Dadash Buniatzade, Ghazanfar Musabekov, and Mirza Davud Huseynov. The party's middle echelon was also decimated. Baghirov's grip on the CPAz ended only after the death of Stalin in 1953. He was removed from all posts and was later arrested. In 1956 he was tried and executed for his crimes. The Baku newspapers published a list of Baghirov's victims, by that time fully rehabilitated.

His successor was Imam Dashdemiroghlu **Mustafayev,** who failed to keep pace with the new drive to assimilate the Russian language, and was removed from office in 1959. Azerbaijan's poor economic performance and widespread corruption led to dismissal of his successor, Veli **Akhundov,** in 1969.

By the mid-1960s the CPAz had become predominantly Azeri (61 percent). Still, Russians and Armenians continued to hold many key posts, and were overrepresented within the party apparatus.

To clean up corruption and improve the plight of Azerbaijan's economy, Haidar **Aliyev** replaced Akhundov as first secretary of the CPAz. His performance was seen as so successful that in 1982 he was promoted to the Politburo of the Communist Party of the Soviet Union in Moscow. His successor, Kamran **Baghirov,** lacked his predecessor's ability to tackle Azerbaijan's recurring problems. His mishandling of the **Nagorno-Karabagh dispute** led to his forced retirement in 1988. He was replaced by Abdurrakhman **Vazirov.**

By the time Vazirov assumed office, Azerbaijan's economic, political, and environmental condition had reached a critical point. In November 1988 large crowds of protesters demonstrated in Baku's Lenin Square. Grievances broadened to include demands for cultural freedom and the cleanup of the environment. In July 1989 the **People's Front of Azerbaijan** (PFAz) formed as the main opposition force to the CPAz and Soviet rule. The PFAz organized a series of strikes and demonstrations calling for Vazirov's removal and secession from the USSR. In January 1990 Moscow dispatched troops to Azerbaijan to regain control of the situation, with bloodshed resulting. In the aftermath of **Black January days,** as many CPAz members publicly burned their party cards in protest against the Soviet invasion, Vazirov was replaced by Ayaz Niyazi **Mutalibov.** In his capacity as head of the party, he presided over the dissolution of the CPAz in September 1991, following the failed coup against Gorbachev in Moscow. *See also* ALIYEV, HAIDAR; BAGHIROV, MIR JAFAR; PEOPLE'S FRONT OF AZERBAIJAN.

CONGRESS OF THE PEOPLES OF THE EAST. An international meeting held in **Baku,** under the auspices of the Communist International, on September 1–8, 1920, in the interval between local uprisings in the Azerbaijani countryside. Delegates came from 38 countries, but the overwhelming majority were from Turkey and Iran, and most were nationalists rather than Communists. The ostensible aim of the congress was to define a program for liberation of the Eastern peoples from European colonialism. Its true intention, however, was to use the revolutionary potential of the East as a trump card in the negotiations that were in progress between Soviet Russia and the liberal-conservative coalition government in Britain.

COTTON CULTIVATION. Cotton has been a major crop in Azerbaijan since its large-scale introduction following the collapse of American cotton exports during the 1860s. Under the Russian administration, cotton was often planted at the expense of food crops. This enforced cultivation of cotton was frequently resisted by farmers, but to little avail. Cotton production steadily increased right up to the Russian Revolution. Following the Soviet takeover, the central government's need to acquire cotton at low, fixed prices led to a further increase in production. Between 1920 and 1922 the amount of land given over to cotton growing doubled. During **World War II,** Azerbaijan produced 500,000 tons of cotton for the war effort. By the 1960s production was up to 2.4 million tons. In the 1970s it reached 5.5 million. The end of the 1980s saw Azerbaijan's environment in a dangerous state due to the extensive cultivation of cotton. Chemical fertilizers, pesticides, and herbicides used to boost production along with salinization of the soil from irrigation had polluted much of Azerbaijan and left dangerously high levels of chemicals in the soil and air of agricultural regions. By 1987 Soviet authorities reported the infant mortality rate in Azerbaijan was 30.5 per 1,000 live births, with high rates of infectious diseases. These high rates were linked to the chemicals used in the cultivation of cotton. By 1989 the concentration of pesticides in Azerbaijan was 20 times the average in the Soviet Union. Azerbaijan has yet to deal effectively with the problems associated with cotton growing and the resultant pollution. *See also* ECONOMY.

CURRENCY. The Russian ruble became the official currency of Azerbaijan with the country's incorporation into the Russian Empire in the 19th century. Following independence in August 1991, there was agitation for a national currency due to fluctuations in the value of the ruble. In addition, Azerbaijan wished to be free of Russian economic domination. In June 1992 a new currency, the manat, began to circulate. The ruble was phased out by July 1, 1992. After a period of hyperinflation in 1994 when the prices were increasing at the rate of 50 percent a month, the manat stabilized and began a slow but steady rise in value in relation to the U.S. dollar. *See also* ECONOMY.

-D-

DAGHESTAN (Land of the Mountains). An autonomous republic within the Russian Federation situated east of the **Caucasus Mountains** and the **Caspian Sea.** With an area of 19,421 square miles (50,300 sq km), it borders Stavropol' Kray, Kalmykia, the Caspian Sea, Azerbaijan, Georgia, and Chechnya. The capital city is Makhachkala. Daghestan's population by the 1989 census was 1,802,000, consisting of 30 ethnic groups of whom 26 percent were Avars; Dargins, 16 percent; Kumyks, 13 percent; Lesgins, 11 percent; Russians, 9 percent; Tabassarans, 4 percent; Nogaiis, 2 percent; Tutuls, 1 percent; Auguls, 1 percent.

Daghestan was penetrated by Russians as early as the 15th century, but was not formally annexed until the 1813 Russo-Iranian Treaty of **Gulistan.** In subsequent decades, Daghestan became the center of the Islamic anticolonial resistance movement that reached its high point under the leadership of **Shamil.** Even after his surrender, a large scale uprising broke out in Daghestan and Chechnya at the beginning of the Russo-Ottoman War in 1877. In the early Soviet period Daghestan was the scene of the 1921 anti-Soviet uprising headed by Imam Gotsinskii. The same year, it received the status of an Autonomous Soviet Socialist Republic. Following the break-up of the Soviet Union, Daghestan remained a republic of the Russian Federation. *See also* CAUCASIA; SHAMIL.

DASHNAKTSUTIUN (ARMENIAN REVOLUTIONARY FEDER-ATION). Founded in 1890 in Tbilisi, the party became the leading political force of the Armenian community in **Caucasia.** The Dashnak ideology was fundamentally nationalist with some elements of moderate socialism. The party's immediate goal was to secure autonomy for the part of eastern Turkey populated by Armenians. Dashnak forms of political actions included individual acts of terrorism and the use of fighting squads, notably in the ethnic clashes of the 1905 revolution in Caucasia. The Dashnaktsutiun's 1907 program accepted as its goal the federal restructuring of **Transcaucasia** on national lines as an autonomous unit within a democratic Russian state. In the period of Armenia's independence, 1918–1920, the Dashnaktsutiun was the ruling party in the republic. *See also* ARMENIANS IN AZERBAIJAN; TATAR-ARMENIAN WAR.

DECEMBER RESCRIPT OF 1846. A decree issued by Tsar Nicholas I (1825–1855) on the recommendation of the viceroy of the Caucasus, Prince Mikhail S. **Vorontsov,** whereby hereditary and inalienable rights to *tuls* (land grants) were awarded to *beys* and *aghas* (Muslim landholders). The decree was intended to raise them to the equivalent of the Russian *dvorianie* (gentry), and to provide safeguards for the corporate rights of the Muslim privileged classes. At the same time, the tsar imposed specified dues and obligations on the peasantry that bore resemblance to serfdom.

DEDE KORKUT, THE BOOK OF. A *dastan* (poetic legend) that records the early history of the **Oghuz Turks,** from whom the **Azeris** trace their lineage. Although recorded in written form not later than the 15th century, *The Book of Dede Korkut* was passed down orally by Turkic nomads from before the 10th century. Its twelve sections are set in Asia Minor and **Caucasia,** and refer to the Black Sea, Trebizond, Georgia, and other local geographic points and persons. Little is known of Dede Korkut himself, the reciter–compiler of the *dastan,* and there have been doubts raised as to whether he really existed. Although since its composition it has acquired Islamic additions to the text, the *dastan* describes much of pre-Islamic life and customs. In the book, family and clan loyalty are paramount, and truthfulness and courage are prized qualities. *See also* LITERATURE, AZERI.

DEMOCRATIC PARTY OF AZERBAIJAN (DPAz, 1917–1920). A political party founded in 1917 in **Iranian Azerbaijan** by Shaikh Muhammad **Khiabani.** Its nucleus was the local branch of Iran's Democratic Party, which was active in the constitutional revolution period. Upon its formation, the DPAz addressed a series of demands to the central government. The party called for the appointment of a provincial governor trusted by the local population, the creation of provincial councils as provided by the Iranian constitution, land redistribution, a convening of the national assembly, equitable parliamentary representation, and an increase in the budgetary allocation for the province of Azerbaijan. These demands displayed a clear autonomist-decentralizing disposition.

The DPAz extended its activities north of the border in 1918 by starting a chapter in **Baku,** where it also published a newspaper, *Azerbaijan.* Its main press organ was the **Tabriz** Persian-language newspaper *Tajaddod* (Renewal). The DPAz had to suspend its activities during the Ottoman occupation of Iranian Azerbaijan in the summer and fall of 1918. After the end of the war, the DPAz became the uncontested political force in the region. In the summer of 1919, it mounted a mass protest campaign against the just concluded Anglo-Iranian Agreement, calling it a colonialist compact, harmful to Tabriz's trading interests. In April 1920, the DPAz launched a revolt against the central government of Iran, blaming it for the failure to observe the constitutional laws of the country. The DPAz government in Tabriz renamed Iranian Azerbaijan **Azadistan** (Land of Freedom) to distance it from the independent Azerbaijani republic under the Baku regime. Yet the Communists' seizure of power across the boundary of the **Araxes River** soon engendered suspicions and apprehensions in the DPAz leadership as to Soviet intentions. While the DPAz kept denying any tendencies toward separatism, it declined to subordinate Azerbaijan to the central government. The Teheran regime resolved to reclaim its control over the province, and Iranian Cossacks entered Tabriz on September 4, 1920. The DPAz was dispersed and Khiabani was killed. *See also* AZADISTAN; IRANIAN AZERBAIJAN; KHI-ABANI, SHAIKH MUHAMMAD; TABRIZ.

DEMOCRATIC PARTY OF AZERBAIJAN (DPAz, 1945–1960). A political organization founded in Soviet-occupied **Iranian Azerbaijan** on September 3, 1945, by Jafar Sayyid **Pishevari,** Ali Shabustari, and Sadeq Padhegani. The name "Democratic" meant to evoke memories of **Khiabani**'s movement of 1917–1920, whose survivors the party wished to attract. Although the Democratic Party absorbed the local chapters of the Iranian Tudeh Party, it rejected sectarianism, aiming to forge as broad based a political force as possible, but under the hegemony of the Communists. Moreover, in contrast to the Tudeh, DPAz emphasized two new issues: the identity of the **Azeris** as a distinct nationality, and the need for the decentralization of Iran. The DPAz Constituent Congress met on October 2, 1945, to adopt a program that called for regional autonomy and the right to national self-determination.

Pishevari was not only the leader of the party, but also the spokesman for its ideology and tactics. In his articles in the newspaper, *Azerbaijan,* he formulated the minimum DPAz demands: education in the Azeri **language,** administrative and economic autonomy, and the formation of a provincial council. In mid-November 1945, the DPAz, with discreet support from Soviet troops, carried out a seizure of power in Azerbaijan by disarming garrisons of the Iranian army. On November 20, the national Constituent Congress adopted a proclamation confirming Azerbaijan's attachment to Iran while asserting its right to freedom and autonomy based on distinct national, linguistic, and cultural characteristics.

Despite assurances that the DPAz was not separatist, its **autonomous government** took steps that were seen as setting Azerbaijan apart from Iran, such as the creation of a national army, indigenization of the civil service, and elevation of Azeri to the status of official language. While the DPAz regime's achievements in building up the native education and cultural life were impressive, they were marred by growing police terror and economic hardships. The withdrawal of Soviet troops from Azerbaijan on May 6, 1946, left the DPAz regime without an outside power's protection. In November, Iranian troops entered the province and put an end to the autonomous government. Some 15,000 refugees, Pishevari and other leaders among them, fled to Soviet Azerbaijan to escape Iranian vengeance. The DPAz continued to exist as an underground organization until it united with the Iranian Tudeh Party in 1960. *See also* AUTONOMOUS GOVERNMENT OF AZERBAIJAN; BIRIYA, MUHAMMAD; IRANIAN AZERBAIJAN; MUHAJIRIN; PISHEVARI, JAFAR SAYYID.

DERBENT KHANATE. A principality in the northernmost part of Azerbaijan bordering with Daghestan, centered on the town of Derbent. Formed in 1747 following the assassination of **Nadir Shah** of Iran, it continued as an independent khanate until occupied by Russian forces in 1796. The Russian annexation was formally recognized by the Treaty of **Gulistan** of 1813. During the 1820s the Derbent khanate was abolished and its territory was incorporated into the Russian province of Derbent.

DERBENT SHIRVANSHAHS. The dynasty that replaced the **Kesranids** as rulers of **Shirvan** and northern Azerbaijan. The dynasty was founded by **Ibrahim I** (d. 1417), whose ancestors had been rulers of the city of Derbent. The Derbent Shirvanshah dynasty ruled from 1382 to 1538 when the troops of the **Safavid** ruler Tahmasp I (1524–1576) occupied Shirvan and annexed it. The last Derbent Shirvanshah, Shanrukh, was captured and taken to **Tabriz** where he was executed in 1538. *See also* SHIRVAN; SHIRVANSHAHS.

DIFAI (DEFENSE). A secret organization formed in 1905 in the city of **Ganja** as a counterterrorist force against the Armenian **Dashnaktsutiun** party. Its founders were local notables, Shafi bey Rustambekov, the brothers Alakpar and Khalil Khasmammadov, Ismail Ziyatkhanov, Nasib bey **Yusufbeyli** (Ussubekov), and Hasan Aghazade. They believed that the Russian authorities were encouraging the Armenians and instigating intercommunal clashes to keep **Transcaucasia**'s inhabitants divided. Accordingly, the Difai directed its efforts against the Russian authorities and carried out assassinatons of several tsarist officials. To blunt the edge of intracommunal violence,

Difai maintained contacts with the Dashnaktsutiun and the Ottoman League of Decentralization. After 1909, its activities ceased and the party disbanded. It was revived following the February 1917 Russian Revolution when it became part of the Executive Committee of Social Organizations (IKOO) in Ganja. *See also* TATAR-ARMENIAN WAR.

DISPLACED PERSONS AND WAR REFUGEES. A major result of the Azerbaijani–Armenian conflict has been the displacement of a substantial part of the **Azeri** population. There are two main groups of persons who had to leave their place of residence because of the conflict: refugees from the **Nagorno-Karabagh dispute** are estimated at 650,000, and those forced to move from the territory of the Armenian Republic number about 200,000. Approximately one out of every nine inhabitants of Azerbaijan is a refugee or displaced person. Of the **Nagorno-Karabagh** refugee population, around 60,000 live in tent camps, 300,000 are housed in schools and public buildings, and close to 300,000 live in towns and villages, with living conditions ranging from independent accommodations in houses and apartments to dugouts and abandoned railway cars.

Statistical data show that the war refugees are among the poorest in the country. Results from a United Nations survey indicate that around 45 percent had not eaten meat in the previous six months. Still, not all of them are poor. In fact, roughly one in four households remains above the poverty line.

In general, the refugees and displaced persons live in small settlements, more often in cities or small towns than in villages. Their presence in unoccupied areas of Azerbaijan has created a range of local problems. As a result of the influx of the refugees, the population in about one-fifth of Azerbaijan's 60 political regions increased by 20 percent, and in six regions by 33 percent. Especially heavy strain has been put on employment conditions, educational systems, and health services. Unlike in some other countries, the Azeri displaced persons do not form a political pressure group.

Virtually all refugees expressed the wish to return home as soon as peace is achieved. Given the extent of destruction and abundance of land mines in occupied territories, a sustainable return will require a large investment in reconstruction efforts. *See also* NAGORNO-KARABAGH DISPUTE.

DUNSTERVILLE, LIONEL C., MAJOR-GENERAL. Commander of the British Expeditionary Force in the **Caucasus** in the summer of 1918. Dunsterville's command was sent to northern Iran in February 1918 to keep an eye on Ottoman movements in **Transcaucasia.** After fighting the Iranian nationalist leader of Gilan province, Mirza Kuchuk Khan, Dunsterville's force captured the **Caspian Sea** port of Enzeli from the Bolshevik Soldiers Soviet which had seized power over the town. While in Enzeli, Dunsterville received a request from the **Central Caspian Dictatorship** for British aid against the advancing Ottoman Turks. The British landed in **Baku** between August 9 and 17 with only three battalions, a battery of field artillery, and some armored cars. The defense of the city by so small a force proved impossible, since the Baku leadership was unable to agree on a course of action and its troops were undisciplined. After sustaining heavy casualties in action against the Ottoman army on the outskirts of Baku, Dunsterville evacuated his force by sea to Iran on September 14, 1918. *See also* AZERBAIJANI DEMOCRATIC REPUBLIC; BAKU COMMUNE; CENTRAL CASPIAN DICTATORSHIP.

-E-

EASTERN TRANSCAUCASIA. The name used jointly for the *guberniias* of **Baku** and Elizavetpol following the mid-19th-century Russian administrative reforms. The formation of these two provinces consolidated the bulk of the **Azeri** populated territory into one block, which would in 1918 be the core of independent Azerbaijan. All the same, the Russian administrative reforms did not create an ethnically homogeneous entity. According to the 1871 census, in the Elizavetpol *guberniia,* approximately one-third of the population were **Armenians,** and the inhabitants of the Baku *guberniia* included an even larger proportion of non-natives—Russians, Lesgins, Armenians, Jews, and others.

ECONOMY. By the standards of the former USSR, Azerbaijan belonged to the middle-range of developed republics. Its economy grew largely as an appendage to Russia, and was oriented primarily to Russian markets and, to a lesser degree, to the markets of neighboring parts of **Transcaucasia.**

After the breakup of the Soviet Union, the Azerbaijani economy experienced a serious decline that started earlier and lasted longer than in many other republics. The major causes of this downturn were disruption of commercial ties to the former USSR (a condition aggravated by upheaval in the neighboring Chechnya), the **Nagorno-Karabagh dispute,** and the collapse of a large part of the state-owned manufacturing sector. Real Gross Domestic Product fell by 23 percent to $730 per capita in 1993, and another 22 percent the next year. By comparison, the 1993 average for Central Asia and Transcaucasia was $848 per capita. In the second half of 1994 Azerbaijan approached the condition of hyperinflation with monthly price increases of 50 percent.

As the result of a series of measures taken by the end of the year—tightening the credit policy, ending the interest-free loans to inefficient state enterprises, elimination of subsidies for bread and gasoline, and adoption of a restrictive state budget—the inflation rate declined dramatically, from 1,664 percent in 1994 to 85 percent in 1995. The exchange rate of the national currency, the manat, which was 4,575 to the U.S. dollar at the end of 1995, rose to 4,098 by the end of the next year. Because of the relative weight of imports in the cost of living index, the stability of the exchange rate contributed significantly to the sharp reduction of the increase in the Consumer Price Index.

Since the breakup of the USSR, inequality in standards of living has increased sharply, resulting in unprecedented stratification in the society. The economic stabilization entailed its costs. The results of the Azerbaijan Survey of Living Conditions indicate that over three-fifths of households were living in poverty at the end of 1995, of which 20 percent belonged to the category of "very poor."

Azerbaijan's medium-term prospects, in the words of a World Bank report, are excellent if several constraints can be overcome. Its human and natural resources place it in a relatively favorable position. It has a well-educated labor force. Agriculture, which accounts for 37 percent of the country's labor force, is the most important sector of the economy, in both output and employment. The expectations are that with the privatization of the agricultural sector its structural weakness and inefficiency will be overcome. But the process of privatization is slow.

Azerbaijan has a diversified industrial sector, although now in serious depression and in need of substantial restructuring. There is a strong enterpreneurial tradition, so far manifested primarily in commercial activities, that survived seven decades of the "command economy."

Azerbaijan's medium-term program, based on macroeconomic progress already achieved, is designed to prepare the country for the prospective oil boom. Oil production was expected to double by the turn of the century, and to quadruple shortly thereafter. The program envisages a strengthening of structural reforms and improvement in the social safety net.

Within this medium-term program, the goals were set at an annual Gross Domestic Product growth in excess of 5.1 percent, a further decline in the annual inflation rate, and a narrowing of the external current account. The improving balance of payment led to further strengthening of the manat from the level of 4,440 per U.S. dollar at the end of 1995 to 3,950 in early 1997. The appreciation reflects the effect of market forces rather than of government decree. These predictions did not, however, foresee the sharp decline in the world oil prices, which fell in 1998 to about $10 per barrel.

As for further strengthening of structural reforms, the areas highest priority are banking, increasing the pace of privatization, phasing out the government's heavy involvement in production, and liberalizing trade. *See also* COTTON CULTIVATION; CURRENCY; OIL INDUSTRY.

EDUCATION. Universal elementary education was introduced in Azerbaijan under the Soviet regime in 1928. The literacy ratio, around 10 percent before the 1917 Revolution, grew impressively—a process facilitated by the switch from the Arabic to the Latin alphabet. By the 1959 census the adult literacy figure reached 97 percent. Also by this date, compulsory eight-year schooling went into effect, and in 1966 the transition to universal secondary education, largely in vocational schools, began.

Another side of the Soviet educational policy was the promotion, especially from the late 1950s on, of Russian-language schools for the **Azeris.** The number of these schools increased steadily for the remainder of the Soviet period, and they remained in existence under the post-1991 independent republic.

Of the institutions of higher learning, the largest and oldest is the Rasulzade (formerly Kirov) State University in **Baku,** founded in 1919. Among other state institutions of this category are the Polytechnic Institute, the Institute of Petroleum and Chemical Industry, the Medical Institute, and the Hajibeyli Conservatory of Music. The post-Soviet period saw the rise of private academic institutions with English as the language of instruction, such as Western and Khazar (Caspian) Universities, both in Baku. Most of the research activity is conducted under the auspices of the Azerbaijani Academy of Sciences, in existence since 1945.

At the present time, Azerbaijan's educational system includes some 1,300 kindergartens, 4,600 primary and secondary schools, 180 technical lyceums, 90 colleges, and 27 institutions of higher learning. The student population at all levels reaches 1,630,000, or more than one-fifth of the Republic's inhabitants. The number of teachers is 266,000, or about 44 percent of all government employees, making education the second-largest sector of employment after agriculture. The national economy may not be able to continue supporting a public education system that employs teachers at the ratio of one to every six students, and education reform is becoming a major issue of the labor market.

EJTIMA-I AMIYYUN (SOCIAL DEMOCRACY). A political organization of Iranian workers in **Baku** founded in 1906 under the guidance of the **Himmat Party**. The organization was initially headed by Nariman N. **Narimanov** and consisted primarily of workers from **Iranian Azerbaijan.** During the **Iranian Constitutional Revolution,** it shifted the focus of its activities to **Tabriz.** The Ejtima-i Amiyyun was succeeded by the **Adalat** Party in 1916. *See also* ADALAT.

ELCHIBEY, ABULFAZ (1939–). A scholar by profession in the field of Middle East studies, Elchibey was also a dissident and political prisoner under the Soviet regime. He became the leader of the **People's Front of Azerbaijan** (PFAz), and second president of the post-Soviet **Republic of Azerbaijan.** In June 1992, he succeeded the former Communist Party head, Ayaz **Mutalibov,** as the first democratically elected president, receiving 59 percent of the vote. Elchibey, a leader without administrative experience, articulated more clearly than any other Azerbaijani public figure the community's historically ingrained aspirations and concerns, which included emancipation from Russia's all-pervading grip, closer relations with Turkey, and closer ties with the **Azeri** population across the Iranian border. He sought to act upon these goals, only to find that they exacted a heavy price and could be mutually exclusive.

Elchibey's regime was unable to turn around the **Nagorno-Karabagh dispute** in which the Azerbaijani forces suffered heavy losses in the winter and spring of 1993. Nor was the **intelligentsia** from the ranks of the PFAz able to run the state independently of the former Soviet elite, the *nomenklatura.* In foreign policy, Elchibey's rapprochement with Turkey did not result in the hoped for scale of assistance for Azerbaijan. His openly voiced concern about cultural rights of Iranian Azeris aroused the distrust of the Teheran government.

In a major reorientation of the politics of oil, Elchibey's regime made overtures to Western companies, concluding an agreement with them on investments and joint exploration of the offshore deposits — a step that displeased Moscow. In June 1993, a military coup of Colonel Surat **Huseynov** forced Elchibey to leave **Baku,** "to avoid fratricidal bloodshed," without formally relinquishing his office. He lost the presidency as the result of the referendum held under the regime of Haidar Aliyev and Huseynov, that emerged from the coup.

Subsequently, Elchibey spent four years in his native village in the Nakhichevan region, returning to Baku in the fall of 1997. In the presidential election season of late 1998, he accused Aliyev of having taken part in founding the Kurdistan Workers Party (PKK), banned by Turkey as a terrorist organization. This allegation brought down on Elchibey a court case for having insulted the dignity of a president of the republic. The case was dropped in early 1999. *See also* PEOPLE'S FRONT OF AZERBAIJAN; REPUBLIC OF AZERBAIJAN.

ELIZAVETPOL. *See* GANJA.

ERIVAN KHANATE. One of the Azerbaijani principalities emerging from the mid-18th-century disintegration of central authority in Iran. In the initial stage of its existence, the khanate remained in close alliance with its stronger neighbor, the Georgian kingdom of Kartli-Kakheti. When the kingdom signed the Georgievsk treaty of submission to Russia in 1783, the Erivan khanate found itself threatened by the growing Russian influence in **Transcaucasia.** It was reclaimed by Iran's ruler Muhammad Agha, and after his death in 1797 the khanate returned under the native rule of Muhammad Khan of Erivan. The 1813 Treaty of **Gulistan** confirmed the khanate as a part of Iran, but with the 1828 Treaty of **Turkmanchai** its territory passed under the sovereignty of Russia. In 1834, the lands of the former khanates of **Erivan** and **Nakhichevan** were joined into the Armenian *Oblast* (district), an administrative unit created to accommodate the influx of Armenian immigrants from Iran and Turkey.

-F-

FATH ALI KHAN OF KUBA (1736–1789). Ruler of the **Kuba Khanate** from 1758 until his death in 1789. Fath Ali Khan had ambitions to repeat the feat of the **Safavids** who had used Azerbaijan as a base for extending their power over Iran. He conquered the **Derbent, Baku,** and **Shirvan** Khanates, and united under his sway the lands of the Caspian coast as far as Ardabil in the south. His actions alarmed Russia, which did not want a strong state in what it considered its future sphere of influence. In 1784 the Russian armies operating against Turkey from the **Caucasus Mountains** forced Fath Ali Khan to relinquish most of his conquests. In 1787 he concluded a mutual protection pact with Irakli II of Georgia against Iranian attempts at recovering the Caucasus. After his death the Kuba Khanate declined and was formally annexed by Russia in the Gulistan Treaty. *See also* KUBA KHANATE.

FLAG, REPUBLIC OF AZERBAIJAN. Azerbaijan's current national flag was originally adopted by the **Azerbaijani Democratic Republic** on September 24, 1918, and flew until the republic was overthrown by the Bolsheviks on April 20, 1920. It was adopted again after Azerbaijan's declaration of independence from the USSR on August 30, 1991. It consists of a horizontal tricolor of blue, red, and green, with a white crescent and star in the center. The three colors symbolize the slogan of the early-20th-century national movement: Turkify, Islamicize, and Modernize. It replaces the flag of the Azerbaijani SSR which consisted of a red field with a gold star, a hammer and sickle, and a blue stripe running along the bottom edge. *See also* AZERBAIJANI DEMOCRATIC REPUBLIC; AZERBAIJANI REPUBLIC; AZERBAIJANI SOVIET SOCIALIST REPUBLIC.

FUZULI, MEHMET SULEYMANOGHLI (1494–1556). One of the most outstanding figures in the classical **literature** of Turkic peoples. A resident of Baghdad, he wrote his major works in **Azeri.** His first patron was Shah **Ismail I** of Iran, and later, when Baghdad passed under Ottoman rule, he tried to gain the favor of Sultan Suleyman I. Fuzuli's famous poetical work *Shikayetnameh* (Book of Complaint) expresses his resentment at not being appointed a court poet in Istanbul. His other famous works are the allegoric romance, *Layla va Majnun,* and two *divans* (collections) of lyrical poetry conveying mystical meaning, one in Azeri, another in Persian. The themes of his poems reappeared in the dramatic and operatic works of the 20th-century Azerbaijani authors. *See also* LITERATURE.

FUYUZAT **(ABUNDANCE).** A literary-artistic journal in existence from 1906 to late 1907, which, by its intellectual standards and breadth of subject matter was comparable to the renowned Istanbul review, *Servet-i Funun*. *Fuyuzat*'s founder and chief contributor was Ali bey **Huseynzade.** He defined the journal's concerns as Turkism, Islam, and European civilization. *Fuyuzat* crusaded for the emancipation of native culture from the double burden of alien influences—the traditional Iranian, and the more recent Russian. The group of writers who contributed to it initiated a trend called "*Fuyuzat* Literature," sometimes also referred to as neoromanticism. Its characteristics included an "art for art's sake" aestheticism, a rich and complex **language,** and a pronounced consciousness of Turkism.

The *Fuyuzat* writers promoted the view that Turkic peoples everywhere should use a single literary **language,** a modified Ottoman. Contributions to *Fuyuzat* were, for the most part, written in that language, often in an elaborate style with an elitist disregard for the average **Azeri** who often could not understand them. In the debate on the literary language, *Fuyuzat* represented the Ottomanizers versus the proponents of the Azeri language. *See also* AZERI LITERATURE; AZARIJI-LAR; HUSEYNZADE, ALI BEY; PRESS.

-G-

GANJA. The second-largest city in Azerbaijan, with a population of 278,000. It is located on the northeastern foot of the Lower Caucasus Range on the Ganjachai River. The city was founded in the fifth century and was later moved to its present site after being destroyed by an earthquake in 1138. Throughout the 12th and 13th centuries it was the major cultural, as well as commercial, center of Azerbaijan. In the course of its history, the city was destroyed repeatedly by Mongols, Turks, and Iranians. In the 18th century it was the capital of the **Ganja Khanate** until being conquered by Russia in 1804 and renamed Elizavetpol. In 1868 it became the capital of Elizavetpol *guberniia*. During the period of the **Azerbaijani Democratic Republic,** the city was occupied first by Ottoman troops, then by the British army, and finally by Bolshevik forces in May 1920. In the 1930s the Soviets changed the city's name to

Kirovabad in honor of the Bolshevik leader Sergei M. Kirov. Since Azerbaijan's declaration of independence from the Soviet Union, the city has returned to its original name.

Today, Ganja is one of the most important industrial centers of Azerbaijan, with light industry consisting of textile and carpet factories and food and cotton processing plants. Heavy industry consists of aluminum foundries and building materials factories. *See also* GANJA KHANATE.

GANJA KHANATE. An Azerbaijani principality in existence in the 18th and early 19th centuries. The Ganja Khanate was situated in the **Kura River** valley, with its capital in the fortress city of **Ganja.** The first khan, Ziyad-Oghli was the hereditary owner of the lands in the Ganja-Shakhverdi region, and declared his khanate independent of Iran in the mid-18th century. In 1804, the khanate was occupied by Russian troops after a heavy show of resistance by Khan Javad who was killed in the final battle. Subsequently, the Ganja Khanate was incorporated into the Russian Empire as Elizavetpol province.

GANJA, TREATY OF (1735). A treaty between Russia and Iran signed on March 10, 1735, near **Ganja.** Under the terms of the treaty, Russia and Iran became allied against the Ottoman Empire, and Russia returned to Iran the captured towns of **Derbent** and **Baku,** as well as their surrounding territories. Both sides also agreed not to enter into any separate negotiations with the Ottoman sultan, and to jointly draw up the terms of the eventual peace treaty with Turkey. They further agreed to observe the terms of the Treaty of Rasht (1732). Under the Rasht agreement, Russia had returned Gilan to Iran and in return Iran had agreed, in the event of the kingdom of eastern Georgia being won back from the Ottomans, to restore it to the Kartlian king, Vakhtang VI. Finally, the treaty confirmed Russia's right of free trade in Iran.

GANJA UPRISING. An uprising against the newly established Soviet regime by the Azerbaijani army units in **Ganja** on May 28, 1920. Some 1,800 troops took over the Muslim sections of Ganja and began to disarm Red Army soldiers. The fighting that followed was heaviest around the railroad station, where Azeri troops attempted to dislodge the Red Army, keeping the rail line open for reinforcements. Large numbers of Red forces arrived by rail and surrounded the city. On May 29, the Reds launched a series of attacks that were repelled with heavy losses. The revolt was finally crushed on May 31. The suppression of the uprising led to several hundred executions in the city and a purge of the Azerbaijani army throughout the country, with numerous officers arrested and some executed.

GASPIRALI (GASPRINSKI) ISMAIL BEY (1851–1914). A Crimean Tatar, one of the founders of **Pan-Turkism.** His newspaper, *Tarjuman* (Interpreter) began publication in 1883 in Bakhchisaray (Crimea) with support from the **Baku** millionaire Zeynal Abdin **Taghiyev.** In response to the dangers of Pan-Slavism, Gaspirali preached the unity of Turkic peoples within the Russian Empire. Although he wrote of one great *qavm* (nation) of all Turks, he stopped short of calling for political action—an unrealistic prospect in any case, given the repressive climate of the epoch. The Turkic unity that he envisaged had spiritual, linguistic, and cultural qualities, expressed in the slogan: "Unity of language, thought, and work."

The first step toward this goal was to be the creation of a literary idiom that served all Turks, from the Balkans to the Great Wall of China. Such a **language,** based on simplified Ottoman, was in fact forged in the columns of the *Tarjuman* and taught in the *jadidist* (modernized) schools. With time, this language would be criticized as artificial and delaying the evolution of vernaculars of Turkic peoples into literary idioms. *See also* JADIDISM; PAN-TURKISM.

GIRDYMAN. A Caucasian Albanian principality located between the **Araxes** and **Kura** Rivers. In the fifth and sixth centuries the principality was a dependency of Sassanid Iran. It flowered under the Mekhranid dynasty during the late sixth and early seventh centuries. The principality reached its apogee under Prince **Javanshir** (638–670), whose descendants inherited the title "Arranshah" (king of **Arran**). The territory of Girdyman was conquered by the Arab caliphate in the beginning of the eighth century, and the Mekhranid dynasty was abolished in A.D. 705. *See also* ARRAN; CAUCASIAN ALBANIA.

GRIBOEDOV, ALEKSANDR S. (1795–1829). A prominent Russian writer, orientalist, and diplomat involved in negotiations with Iran over Azerbaijan. Although as a writer Griboedov represented the Enlightenment trend as shown in his famous play *Woe from Wit,* and had links to the liberal-inclined Decembrist movement, as a diplomat he was committed to Russian expansion in the Middle East. "Respect for Russia and its demands" was his guiding principle in dealing with Iran. He was a chief architect of the 1828 **Turkmanchai Treaty** that completed the Russian conquest in Azerbaijan and assured economic penetration of Iran. Appointed the ambassador to Iran, he met his death the next year at the hands of an angry mob breaking into the Russian embassy compound. *See also* RUSSO-IRANIAN WAR, SECOND (1826–1828).

GULISTAN, TREATY OF (1813). Peace settlement between Iran and Russia that ended the First **Russo-Iranian War** of 1804–1813. The treaty provided for the cession of vast tracts of Iranian territory to the Russian Empire—**Daghestan,** Georgia with the Sheragel province, Imeretia, Guria, Mingrelia, and Abkhazia, as well as the Azerbaijani khanates of **Karabagh, Baku, Sheki, Shirvan, Kuba, Derbent,** and **Talysh.** A special feature of the treaty was Russia's involvement in Iranian succession politics by their commitment to assist the heir to the throne chosen by the shah to retain his position against attempts "from outside to deprive him thereof." Should discord occur among sons of the shah, Russia would refrain from intervening unless "the shah himself requests it." *See also* RUSSO-IRANIAN WAR, FIRST (1804–1813); RUSSO-IRANIAN WAR, SECOND (1826–1828); TURKMANCHAI, TREATY OF (1828).

-H-

HAJIBEYLI, UZEIR (1885–1948). The leading 20th-century Azerbaijani composer and founder of the national opera, active also in the fields of **literature** and political journalism, notably in the pre-Soviet period. In 1907 he composed the first Azerbaijani opera, *Layla va Majnun* based on the poetic work of **Fuzuli.** Produced the next year in **Baku,** the opera met with great success and Hajibeyli subsequently composed a series of operas as well as musical comedies. In most cases he was also librettist. He used motives of the national musical heritage extensively in his art. In the Soviet period, Hajibeyli extended his work to the field of musical education and organization of musical life in Azerbaijan.

HAJINSKI, MAMMAD HASAN (1875–1931). An engineer by training and one of the founding members of the **Himmat Party** in 1904. Hajinski was also coeditor of the leftist weekly *Takammul* (Perfection) that appeared in the years 1906–7. Following the February 1917 Russian Revolution, Hajinski became the head of the executive committee of the Council of Muslim Public Associations. He was part of the Azeri component of the Transcaucasian delegation of the **Trebizond Peace Talks** in March 1918, and again at the Batum Peace Conference in May 1918. Following Azerbaijan's declaration of independence from Russia in May 1918, Hajinski became the minister of the interior for the **Azerbaijani Democratic Republic.** His attempts to preserve Azerbaijan's independence by placating the Bolsheviks led to his dismissal from that post in 1920 and his reassignment as the minister of commerce and industry. The resignation of Nasib bey **Yusufbeyli**'s government in April 1920, gave Hajinski the opportunity to form a cabinet more acceptable to Moscow and thus avert a Red Army invasion of Azerbaijan. However, his efforts were too late, and on April 28, 1920, the Democratic Republic was overthrown by the Bolsheviks. *See also* AZERBAIJANI DEMOCRATIC REPUBLIC; HIMMAT PARTY.

HALIL PASHA, KUT. Ottoman general, and a young uncle of the generalissimo, Enver Pasha. At the onset of **World War I,** Halil was given the task of sweeping through northern Iran, capturing **Baku,** and clearing the Caspian coast of Russian forces. Because of inadequate forces at his disposal, this campaign was unsuccessful. Later, in 1916, he scored a major victory over the British at Kut al-Amara in Iraq, after which he was promoted to commander of the Eastern Army Group. In the last months of the war, the units under his command occupied Iranian Azerbaijan, and by September 15, 1918, succeeded in driving the British expeditionary force from Baku. After the end of the war Halil was arrested on orders of the Ottoman sultan. He escaped and offered his services to the Nationalists under Mustafa Kemal Pasha. The Turkish leader sent Halil on a mission to **Transcaucasia** to arrange for military assistance from Soviet Russia. By December 1919 he had arrived in Azerbaijan and established contact with both the Bolshevik Regional Committee and the Azerbaijani government for the purpose of maintaining an open corridor between Anatolia and Russia. While in Azerbaijan Halil Pasha was active in preparing the way for the Soviet takeover of the country in April 1920. *See also* AZERBAIJANI DEMOCRATIC REPUBLIC; WORLD WAR I AND AZERBAIJAN.

HIMMAT **(ENDEAVOR).** A clandestine newspaper published in **Baku** by a group of Muslim Social-Democrats. The first issue appeared in

October 1904, and was printed in the Azeri **language.** The paper's motto, which appeared on its masthead, was the Arabic proverb, "Joint efforts of men will move mountains." The paper called for instruction in the native language, improvement in the status of women, and the spread of education as the way to progress. Six editions were published before mid-February 1905, when the police seized the publication's printing equipment. *See also* HIMMAT PARTY.

HIMMAT PARTY. A Social Democratic organization formed in **Baku** in 1904 by young Azeri activists. Their number included M. A. **Rasulzade,** S. M. Effendiyev, R. Movsumov, A. J. Akhundov, and M. H. **Hajinski,** some of whom had links to the Russian Social Democrats. In 1905 the group was joined by Meshadi A. **Azizbekov** and Nariman N. **Narimanov,** members of the Russian Social-Democratic Workers Party (RSDWP), who reinforced the leadership of the Himmat at a time when its following grew impressively as the Russian Revolution gained momentum. No longer confining itself to the Baku oil region, the Himmat branched out to provincial towns and even established cells in **Daghestan** and Transcaspia.

The Himmat's relationship to the Russian Social Democracy defies any clearcut definition. Soviet authors emphasized that the Azeri organization in 1905 became affiliated with the RSDWP. The affiliation was, however, on no higher level than the Baku Committee of the RSDWP, which for its part granted the Himmat an autonomous status, an exception to the cardinal principle that party chapters must be formed not on ethnic but on territorial bases.

For all its links with the RSDWP, the Himmat failed to evolve into a centralized, closely knit entity on the Bolshevik pattern. Instead, it continued to operate as a loose association of individuals inclined to radicalism but concerned itself less with doctrine than with action.

When the government resorted to harsh repressions in mid-1907, the Himmat lost its following as quickly as it had gained it. Some of its leaders were arrested and others took refuge in Iran, and by the end of the year the Himmat was a mere shadow of an organized force.

Ten years later, on March 3, 1917, the Himmat was revived by Narimanov and Azizbekov, but it failed to recapture its following in the face of competition from the **Musavat Party.** The Azeri socialists soon split into the Bolshevik and the Menshevik factions, and their role in the politics of independent Azerbaijan remained marginal. On February 11, 1920, the Bolshevik Himmat merged with the **Communist Party of Azerbaijan.** *See also HIMMAT.*

HUSEYNOV, MIRZA DAVUD (1894–1938). One of the leaders of the **Himmat Party**, he later became a member of the Regional Committee of the Russian Communist Party (Bolshevik). Subsequently, he was elected chairman of the Central Committee of the **Communist Party of Azerbaijan** (Bolshevik) in 1920. Following the overthrow of the **Azerbaijani Democratic Republic,** he became a member of the **Azrevkom.** Later he was the commissar of finances in the Azerbaijani Soviet of People's Commissars. Huseynov became a victim of the Stalinist purges in the late 1930s and was executed in 1938. *See also* COMMUNIST PARTY OF AZERBAIJAN; HIMMAT PARTY.

HUSEYNOV, SURAT. Originally a wealthy textile entrepreneur from eastern Azerbaijan. Huseynov used money from his rug manufacturing business to gather Azeri and Russian soldiers into a well-paid military formation that he sent to the fighting in **Nagorno-Karabagh.** Impressed by his services, President **Abulfaz Elchibey** made him a colonel in the Azerbaijani Army.

After the military situation in **Nagorno-Karabagh** deteriorated, Elchibey put part of the blame on Huseynov and dismissed him. In revenge, Huseynov started a revolt in June 1993 in the city of **Ganja.** He then led his followers in a march on **Baku,** forcing Elchibey to leave the capital. Upon Elchibey's departure Haidar **Aliyev** assumed the presidency and named Huseynov prime minister. On October 3, 1994, Aliyev declared a state of emergency in the face of an uprising in Ganja by a paramilitary police unit. He accused Huseynov of being linked to the uprising, which was crushed on October 5, and the next day dismissed Huseynov from office. Huseynov fled to Russia and joined a group of political émigrés centered around Ayaz **Mutalibov.** On insistence of the Azerbaijani government he was delivered in 1998 to Baku, where he was tried to treason and in the next year sentenced to life imprisonment. *See also* ELCHIBEY; REPUBLIC OF AZERBAIJAN.

HUSEYNZADE, ALI BEY (1864–1941). A leading proponent of **Pan-Turkism** in Azerbaijan. As a medical student in St. Petersburg he became impressed with the Pan-Slavic movement, and in 1889 he moved to Istanbul to promote the formation of its equivalent among the Turks of the Ottoman state. Here he became one of the founding members of the Itthad-i Osmaniyye (Ottoman Union), an underground group in opposition to the regime of Sultan Abdul Hamid II. His efforts at inspiring a Pan-Turkic movement in Ottoman Turkey met with limited success, and on the eve of the Russian Revolution of 1905 he returned to **Baku.** The same year he began to write for the newly established **Azeri** newspaper *Hayat* (Life), where he exerted a growing influence over a large segment of the **intelligentsia.** In the pages of *Hayat,* he spelled out for the first time what was to become a famous slogan, "Turkify, Islamicize, Europeanize," subsequently adopted and popularized, in slightly modified form, by the Ottoman Turkish writer, Ziya Gokalp. This slogan became a rallying cry of Turkism in the Ottoman state. Huseynzade expounded on the meaning of his slogan in the literary journal *Fuyuzat* (Abundance), which he founded in 1906 with financial backing of Zaynal Abdin **Taghiyev.**

Huseynzade inveighed against the spirit of parochialism, which he feared could one day engender the idea that the Azeris were a nation of their own, separate from other Turks. He made it clear that he envisioned a national destiny for his compatriots in union with the Ottoman state, which he termed the spiritual and political head of the Islamic world. He was opposed to the use of Azeri as the literary **language** instead of Ottoman. After the **Young Turkish Revolution** of 1908, he moved to Istanbul where he became a university professor. He remained in Turkey for the rest of his life. In the last phase of **World War I,** he advocated the union of the Turkic and Muslim areas of **Transcaucasia** with the Ottoman state in the form of a viceroyalty. *See also* FUYUZAT; LITERATURE; PAN-TURKISM.

-I-

IBRAHIM I (d. 1417). Ruler of **Shirvan** and the founder of the Derbent **Shirvanshah** dynasty. His rule extended from 1382 to 1417. Ibrahim I became a vassal of Tamerlane and supported him against Tokhtamysh of the Golden Horde and the Ottomans. After Tamerlane's death, he became a vassal of the state of the **Qara-Qoyunlu** federation in southern Azerbaijan in 1410. In exchange for his fealty, Ibrahim I was given the lands of **Sheki** and **Derbent** by Qara Yusuf of the Qara-Qoyunlu. *See also* DERBENT SHIRVANSHAHS; QARA-QOYUNLU.

ILDIGUZIDS. An Atabeg dynasty in Azerbaijan and northern Iran from 1136 to 1225. It was founded by **Shams al-Din Ildiguz** (1136–1174), who extended his authority over southern Azerbaijan, part of northern Azerbaijan, and the northwestern parts of Iran. Through their domination of Azerbaijan, the Ildiguzids came to control the Iraqi **Seljuk** sultanate. When the Khwarizm shah Tekish ended the Seljuk sultanate in 1194, the Ildiguzids retained authority in Azerbaijan as the vassals of Khwarizm. After suffering the devastation of the Mongol invasion in 1220–22 the Ildiguzid state fell to the armies of Jalal al-Din of Khwarizm in 1225.

INTELLIGENTSIA. A social force as much as a cultural phenomenon, was the emergence of the native intelligentsia, brought forth by the contact of two civilizations—the European as represented by Russia, and the traditional Islamic. As a group, the intelligentsia shared the set of beliefs, values, and opinions that made them the conduit for European ideas, and in time, the main agent for change within **Azeri** society. In striking disproportion to their numbers, they were destined to have an increasingly greater impact on Azerbaijani history from the mid-19th century on. Initially, the men who made up the intelligentsia were, by virtue of their employment in the tsarist military or civil service, frequently exposed to the Russian environment. Their numbers grew after the **December Rescript** of 1846, when the doors to government positions were opened to the natives of **Transcaucasia.** In the later part of the 19th century, as the civil service was increasingly purged of the Muslim element, the intelligentsia became dominated by graduates of Russian universities and the Transcaucasian teacher seminaries in Gori and Tbilisi. In fact, by the turn of the century, schoolteachers, some of whom took to journalism, were one of the intelligentsia's largest professional components.

In the 19th century, the intelligentsia's main concerns were the spread of enlightenment, modernized education, and the growth of social communications. With the 1905 Russian Revolution, the intelligentsia assumed political leadership of the Azeri community and gradually developed ideas of statehood that found implementation in the independent **Azerbaijani Democratic Republic** of 1918–1920. Under the early Soviet period, a segment of the intelligentsia gave a guarded endorsement to the Communist experiment at modernization, especially in the field of education and in promotion of the national culture. The intelligentsia was the special target of the Stalin purges of the late 1930s, a trauma from which it recovered only in the closing period of the Soviet regime. Members of the intelligentsia intitiated the Azeri dissident movement, and later founded the **People's Front of Azerbaijan.** *See also* EDUCATION; JADIDISM, *PRESS.*

IRANIAN AZERBAIJAN. The region of northwestern Iran, known as Iranian Azerbaijan, consists of the territories between the **Caspian Sea,** Lake Urmia, and the border of the **Azerbaijani Republic.** This area has historically been considered a part of Azerbaijan that was divided by the 1828 Treaty of **Turkmanchai** ending the Second **Russo-Iranian War.** Under the treaty, Fath Ali Shah of Iran renounced his sovereignty over Azerbaijan north of the **Araxes River** in return for peace. These territorial concessions legitimized what the Russian Empire had already conquered. Yet, the Russian conquest did not sever the bonds between the two parts of Azerbaijan. The coming of the industrial age to Russian-held Azerbaijan in the late 19th century increased contacts as **Azeris** from Iran migrated to work in the **Baku** oil fields. Most of these workers were unskilled and worked for a few months each year before returning home. The Russian Revolution of 1905 sent shock waves through Iran that gave rise to the **Iranian Constitutional Revolution** of 1906–1911. The opposition to the **Qajar** absolutism was most active in Iranian Azerbaijan, neighbor to the revolutionized Russia.

In 1908, when Shah Muhammad Ali tried to abrogate the 1906 constitution of Iran, Azerbaijan's main city, **Tabriz,** rose in armed revolt. A major center of the constitutional movement, Tabriz was suppressed by Russian military intervention in 1909, and again in 1912. The Russian occupation that followed in effect brought the two parts of Azerbaijan under the control of one power.

In the last months of **World War I,** the Ottoman troops occupied both Iranian and Russian Azerbaijan, opening the prospect of a union of the divided land under the auspices of Turkey. The Ottoman defeat and surrender put an end to such expectations. The **Azerbaijani Democratic Republic** accepted the 1914 border of Russia as its southern frontier.

The advent of the Pahlavi dynasty's rule in Iran marked an intensification of the assimilationist drive in Iranian Azerbaijan, and the suppression of Azeri **language** education and publishing activity. Economically, under the first of the Pahlavi shahs, Reza, Azerbaijan fared poorly. In addition to the decline of trade and labor migrations with the northern neighbor, the Pahlavi regime's centralization of commerce in the capital dealt a heavy blow to Tabriz. The plight of the Azerbaijani economy worsened further due to the taxation policy under which provinces contributed to the center much more than they received in return.

Mindful of the Soviet threat and local regionalism, in 1937 the Pahlavi regime subdivided the bulk of the Azeri populated area into two *ostans* (provinces), Eastern and Western Azerbaijan, with capitals in Tabriz and Rezaiyeh (formerly Urmia), repectively. Western Azerbaijan included a large Kurdish minority.

During **World War II,** the Soviet Union and Britain occupied Iran to prevent the possibility of disrupting the flow of war supplies to the USSR. In the last year of the occupation, the Soviet Union provided support to the autonomist **Democratic Party of Azerbaijan** (DPAz), and helped to create the **Autonomous Government of Azerbaijan** in 1945. With Soviet assistance and guidance, Iranian Azerbaijan experienced an impressive, if brief, revival of native literature, press, and education. Under pressure from the United Nations Security Council, Soviet troops pulled out on May 6, 1946. In November 1946 Iranian troops entered Iranian Azerbaijan, putting an end to the Autonomous Government of Azerbaijan.

Brutal retribution followed, and the Persianization policy returned with a vengeance. In the 1970s, Azerbaijan began to experience impressive economic growth, sharing in Iran's profits from the oil boom. Toward the end of the decade, Azerbaijan became a major center of the protest movement against the shah's regime. In December 1979, following the Iranian revolution, Tabriz was the scene of a brief mutiny against the centralization policies of the new Teheran regime toward the provinces.

Today, Iranian Azerbaijan has a solid majority of Azeris with an estimated population of at least 15 million (over twice the population of the Azerbaijani Republic). Azeris account for over 85 percent of the Turkic-speaking peoples of Iran, with large concentrations in the cities of Qum and Teheran. The major Azeri cities in Iranian Azerbaijan are Tabriz, Ardabil, Zanjān, Khoi, and Maragheh. *See also* AZADISTAN; DEMOCRATIC PARTY OF AZERBAIJAN (1945–1960).

IRANIAN CONSTITUTIONAL REVOLUTION (1906–1911). The second of the upheavals affecting Azerbaijan in the period of rapid changes that started with the Russian Revolution of 1905. The turmoil in Russia left its impact on Iran in two important ways: it temporarily paralyzed the tsardom's ability for military intervention abroad, and it provided the Iranians with an example that encouraged them to launch their own reforms. Pressures for change had been mounting for many years under the **Qajar** regime, whose hallmarks became stagnation, corruption, and backwardness. At the same time, Britain and Russia, competing for economic influence over Iran, gradually reduced the country to the status of a semicolony.

The crisis in Iran came to a head in December 1905, when the Russian Revolution had already crested. A long series of disturbances forced the shah, Muzaffar al-din, to yield to popular demands, much as Nicholas II had been forced to do in Russia. On August 5, 1906, he signed a law promulgating a constitution under which the Majlis (parliament) would be elected on the basis of a restricted franchise that heavily benefited the interests of the clergy and merchants. These concessions led to calls for the broadening of reforms, and those who were anxious to carry the revolution further began to organize. Mushrooming political associations grew particularly strong in the **Tabriz** province.

This economically advanced region of Iran became the stronghold of the constitutional movement because of its proximity to revolutionized Russia, and Russian Azerbaijan in particular. In **Baku,** the mass of immigrant laborers from Iran became exposed to the agitation of the **Himmat Party,** and in 1906 the first organization of Iranian workers, **Ejtima-i Amiyyun** was set up in Baku and soon branched out to Tabriz.

The fate of the Iranian revolution was not the concern of the socialists alone, and support came from other quarters and in different forms. Intellectual contacts were extensive, and the Baku newspapers that circulated in the Tabriz province were instrumental in stimulating interest in Russian transformations. The Iranian upheaval found ample echoes in the literature of Russian Azerbaijan, most notably in the poetry of Alekpar **Sabir,** the bard of Azeri Sturm und Drang.

The violent phase of the Iranian revolution began in June 1908 when the new shah, Muhammad Ali, staged a coup to restore the absolutist regime. The result was a civil war, as some provincial centers, foremost among them Tabriz, refused to acquiesce to the shah's seizure of power. This new turn of the Iranian upheaval coincided with the wave of post-1907 repressions in Russia—revolutionaries, including Himmatists, migrated across the Iranian border joining the defense of Tabriz against the troops of the shah.

The fall of the city did little to salvage his throne. Another rebel force that included a contingent of Caucasian volunteers moved from Gilan to Teheran. On July 16, 1909, Muhammad Ali renounced the crown in favor of his 12-year-old son, Ahmad. The constitution was restored under the regency of Asad ul Mulk.

The second constitutional period was marked by activities of the émigrés from Baku, and the growing significance of the Azeri-dominated Democratic Party of Iran. It came to an end in January 1912, and by that time the Russian forces effectively controlled northern Iran. The occupation was to have been a temporary arrangement, but the Russian troops remained in Iran until the overthrow of the tsardom in 1917. *See also* IRANIAN AZERBAIJAN; TABRIZ.

ISLAM IN AZERBAIJAN. Islam became the religion of the formerly Zoroastrian, and in Caucasian Albania Christian, population of Azerbaijan in the wake of the Arab conquest in the seventh century. The borderland character of the country accounted for the spread of heresies and the practice of *taqiya,* the dissimulation including apostasy, under compulsion.

Of the two branches of Islam, Shiism was established in the dominant position under the early Safavids, who saw it as an integrating force for their kingdom. Yet, unlike in other parts of Iran, in Azerbaijan north of the **Araxes River** there remained a large number of adherents to Sunnism. The Russian estimates of the 1830s showed that the ratio of Shiites to Sunnis was almost even, but figures for the 1860s indicated that the number of Sunnis had markedly declined. It subsequently stabilized at the level in which the Shi'ite Twelvers of the Jafarite rite held the majority of 2:1. The decrease in the proportionate strength of the Sunni element resulted from their emigration to Turkey after the final suppression of **Shamil's** movement in the **Caucasus.** Sectarian divisions had some impact on cultural, and to some extent political, orientation of the **Azeris,** with the Shi'a majority maintaining links to Iran, and the Sunnis gravitating toward Turkey.

In the Soviet period, strenuous, and at times brutal, efforts were made to uproot Islam among the Azeris. While Islam was greatly weakened as a religion, it remained strong as a way of life—a system of traditions, customs, and prohibitions. The visible manifestations of Islamic identity, such as observance of the Five Pillars of Islam (Profession of Faith, Almsgiving, the Pilgrimage to Mecca, the Ramadan Fast, and the Five Daily Prayers) came into disuse, except for Alms-giving. Likewise, polygamy, forbidden by law, disappeared entirely, and women's veiling and seclusion ended. Even so, Azerbaijani marriages were often arranged, and men and women seldom married outside of the community. Azeris maintained strong kinship loyalties, rarely emigrated, especially to non-Muslim republics, refused to eat pork, and only slowly succumbed to the attractions of alcohol. In general, the population of Muslim regions of the USSR proved to be resistant to cultural assimilation by Russia.

The last antireligious campaign ended with the downfall of Khrushchev, and with time, signs of the Islamic reawakening began to appear. In the late 1970s, according to Soviet sources, approximately one thousand clandestine houses of prayer were in use and some three hundred holy places as destinations of pilgrimages were designated. These could be viewed as having paved the way for the opening of hundreds of mosques in the next decade. Although few observers agreed on the depth and extent of this reawakening, Soviet surveys indicated that, statistically, the level of religiosity was highest in southern districts, and around **Baku,** i.e. in the solidly Shi'a parts of the country.

While the shock waves of the Iranian Revolution reawakened religious sentiments, the open revival came only with the collapse of the Soviet Union. High-ranking officials began to appear at religious festivities, and politicians were courting believers. Iranian clerics set about helping to restore religious life in the Republic of Azerbaijan, a task in which they faced competition from secular Turkey. With support from Teheran, mosques were rebuilt or restored, and future clerics were invited to study in Iran.

Linked to the religious impact of Iran was the emergence in 1992 of a political association, the Islamic Party of Azerbaijan. Its membership soon reached an estimated number of 50,000, mainly in villages around Baku. In 1995 the leader of the party, Aliakram Aliyev, was arrested, and his organization was denied reregistration on the grounds that it was receiving financial support from Iran, and its members were suspected of spying for Iran. In May of the same year all Islamic organizations, as well as mosques, were subordinated to the Muslim Spiritual Board. In 1996 the Parliament adopted a law banning the activities of foreign missionaries and requiring that local religious communities register with centers of traditional religious organizations. These restrictions were justified by the need to prevent the exploitation of religion for political purposes by foreign emissaries. As for the main political parties of Azerbaijan, progovernment and opposition alike, their programs agree in upholding full separation of religion and state.

For all the secularism of the political elite, the overwhelming majority of Azeris are known to identify themselves as Muslims, even though few of them observe the prohibitions and requirements of Islam. One set of figures recently made available estimates the proportion of most ardent believers to be less than a tenth of the population, slightly greater than the proportion of declared atheists, with the balance falling into the category of those who consider Islam as a way of life and a fundamental part of their national identity. *See also* REPUBLIC OF AZERBAIJAN.

ISMAIL I (1487–1524). The founder of the **Safavid dynasty** who ruled Iran from 1501 to 1524. Ismail I came from a prominent family from Ardabil in southern Azerbaijan, and emerged as a political leader while still a young man. As the shah of Iran he made Twelver Shi'ism the state religion of his domains. Ismail I wrote poetry under the pen name Khatai, and is regarded as a major figure in Azeri **literature.** *See also* SAFAVID DYNASTY.

ITTIFAQ (THE UNION OF RUSSIAN MUSLIMS). This organization bringing together the Muslim peoples of the Russian Empire was created at the First All-Russian Muslim congress held in Nizhni Novgorod on August 15, 1905. The congress included delegates from the Crimea, the northern Caucasus, **Transcaucasia,** Kazan, the Urals, Turkestan, and Siberia who met to determine which organizational form the Muslim movement in Russia should assume. The Transcaucasian delegation included Ali Mardan bey **Topchibashi,** who became deputy to the chairman of the congress. By the end of the meeting the moderate faction had prevailed and the decision was made to create a Muslim union instead of a political party. The Ittifaq set for itself the following objectives:

1. The union of Muslims in Russia within one movement.
2. The establishment of a constitutional monarchy based on proportional representation of nationalities.
3. The legal equality of the Muslim and Russian populations and abrogation of all laws and administrative practices discriminatory to Muslims.
4. The cultural and educational progress of Muslims.

At the Third All-Russian Muslim Congress in August 1906, a decision was reached to transform the Ittifaq into a political party representing all of the Muslims of the Russian Empire. The party's platform was similar to that of the liberal Russian Constitutional Democrats (Kadets) with additional emphasis on issues relating to Muslim national and religious equality. The Ittifaq was represented in the First State Duma in May 1906, and Caucasian Muslims, among them Topchibashi, Adil Ziyatkhanov, Alakpar Khasmammadov, and Abdurrahman Haqverdiyev, took their seats. When the First Duma was dissolved three months later, the election laws were altered to reduce the representations of non-Russians. In the Third Duma, whose largely conservative membership was at last acceptable to the tsardom, the Transcaucasian Muslims were represented by only one deputy, Khasmammadov. Following the July 1907 Stolypin Reaction, the Ittifaq virtually dissolved itself.

ITTIHAD (UNION) PARTY. A political party comprising religious and conservative elements of **Azeri** society. The Ittihad (Rusyada Musulmanliq Ittihad) was formed in September 1917 from a union of the **Baku**-based *Rusyada Musulmanliq* (Muslims in Russia) and Ittihad-Islam. The newly formed party headed by Karabey **Karabeyov** was **Pan-Islamist** and accepted the *Shari'a* (holy law of Islam) as the guiding principle in political action. It rejected Azerbaijani nationalism and Turkism in favor of a vision of a democratic and decentralized Russian republic. The Ittihad appealed chiefly to the Azeri peasantry, who gave the party eight percent of the Muslim vote in elections to the Constituent Assembly in November 1917. Although originally a conservative party, the Ittihad had evolved into a quasi-leftist force by late 1919 and was willing to ally itself with the Bolsheviks in early 1920. Its leaders announced their support for communist ideas as long as they did not conflict with Muslim religious beliefs. The Ittihad was for the most part attracted to the Bolsheviks' hostility to nationalism. This attitude made them the natural political opponents of the **Musavat,** and the antagonism between the two groups was a major feature of Azerbaijani domestic politics in the independence period. Following the overthrow of the **Azerbaijani Democratic Republic** the Ittihad disbanded itself, advising its members to join the Communist Party. Yet, soon after the April 28 coup, many Ittihadists took part in the anti-Soviet uprisings of 1920. *See also* AZERBAIJANI DEMOCRATIC REPUBLIC.

-J-

JADIDISM. A movement among the Muslim **intelligentsia** of the Russian Empire to modernize the educational programs of the *maktabs* (Muslim elementary schools) and bring them in line with European teaching practices. *Maktabs,* installed in mosque compounds, combined religious instruction with reading, writing, and arithmetic. Learning was usually by rote. Overall, the reputation of the *maktabs* was low and so was the literacy rate of the Muslim population. The conservative elements among the Muslims of the Russian Empire resisted the learning of the Russian language and modern instruction methods since it was feared that this would lead to the Christianization of children. To allay conservative fears, the Jadidists sought to improve rather than undermine the curricula at traditional learning establishments.

This New Method (*usul-i jadid*) retained religious instruction and the study of the Quran but discouraged rote learning. Science, geography, and modern languages were added, as well as contemporary Turkic. The method originated among the Volga Tatars and spread to the other Muslim populated parts of the Russian Empire. In Azerbaijan, it met with opposition from Iranian-oriented Shi'ites and conservative educators who followed the *usul-i qadim* (Old Method) and were known as Qadimists. The Jadidist movement in Azerbaijan was the first manifestation of **Azeri** involvement in the intellectual ferment affecting the Muslim community outside of **Transcaucasia.** *See* also EDUCATION; INTELLIGENTSIA; SHIRVANI, SAYYID, AZIM.

JAVANSHIR (d. 670). Prince of the Mekhranid dynasty and ruler of **Caucasian Albania** (638–670). During his reign, the Arabs began their conquest of Caucasian Albania and Javanshir fought the Arabs at al-Qadisiyah (637) on the side of the Sassanid forces of Iran. In 660 he concluded a treaty with the Byzantine Empire against the Arab caliphate, but in 667, under threat of attack from the Arabs in the south and the Khazars in the north, he agreed to become a vassal of the Caliphate. In 670 Javanshir was murdered by his feudal lords who resented his accumulation of power.

JAVID HUSEYN, (1882–1941) Pen name of Huseyn Abdullahoghli Rasizade, one of the most outstanding writers of 20th-century Azerbaijan. Born in **Nakhichevan,** he received his education in **Tabriz** and Istanbul in the **Young Turkish** period. Huseyn Javid began with classicist lyrical poetry, but became known primarily as a playwright . With his versified tragedies on philosophical and historical themes, launched the trend of neoromanticism in the pre-Soviet period of Azeri **literature.** He continued writing historical dramas in the Soviet period , but became one of the nost notable victims of the Stalin purges. His exile and death in Siberia were regarded as symbolic of the Stalin era suppression of the independent-minded Azeri literature. *See also* LITERATURE.

-K-

KARABAGH KHANATE. A principality in Azerbaijan founded by Panah Ali Khan in 1747. The khanate achieved its independence from Iran following the assassination of the Iranian ruler **Nadir Shah.** The Karabagh Khanate was located between the **Araxes** and **Kura Rivers,** and periodically extended its influence over the khanates of **Ganja, Erivan, Nakhichevan,** and Ardabil. It also included the largely Armenian-populated mountainous region, **Nagorno-Karabagh.** In 1805 Karabagh signed a treaty accepting a vassalage relationship with Russia. In 1822, the khanate was abolished and replaced by a Russian military administration.

KARABEYOV, KARABEY ISMAILOGHLI (1874–1953). Rightwing, **Pan-Islamist** political figure in pre-Soviet Azerbaijan. By profession a medical doctor, he began his political life in 1905 by joining the **Ganja**-based **Difai** Party. After the **Young Turkish Revolution,** he spent two years in Istanbul, but returned to Azerbaijan on the eve of **World War I.** Following the overthrow of the tsardom, Karabeyov became the leader of the Pan-Islamic **Ittihad** Party, opposed to nationalism in general, and to the **Musavat** in particular. Under the Soviet regime, he was sent to prison camp in the 1920s, and again in the late 1930s. *See also* PAN-ISLAMISM; ITTIHAD (UNION) PARTY.

KASPII **(THE CASPIAN).** A Russian-language newspaper published in **Baku** from the late 19th to the early 20th century. Its owner was Zeynal Abdin **Taghiyev,** and the editor Ali Mardan bey **Topchibashi** (Topchibashev), was a lawyer with close links to Russian liberals. *Kaspii* agitated for such reforms as the improvement of native Muslim educational institutions, access for Muslims to positions in the civil service, and greater access to land ownership for peasants. It gradually attempted to speak for all of the Muslims of the Russian Empire, and expressed **Pan-Turkish** and **Pan-Islamist** sentiments. *See also* LITERATURE, AZERI; PRESS.

KASRAVI, AHMED (1890–1946). A leading historian of **Iranian Azerbaijan,** he is also recognized as the most controversial of modern Iranian thinkers of the 1920s and 1930s. His major concern was the transformation of multiethnic Iran into an integrated nation. Kasravi's *Tarikh-i Hijdah Saleh-i Azarbaijan* (Eighteen Years of History of Azerbaijan) was intended to prove that the fate of Azerbaijan was inextricably tied with the destiny of Iran. He believed that Iran owed its weakness to lack of internal cohesion. Among the forces working for this condition were linguistic differences, which he considered as harmful as tribal loyalties. He believed in the intrinsically Iranian character of the Azeris, and that the true national language of Azerbaijan was Azari, an ancient dialect of the Iranian family of languages. These beliefs formed the basis of what became known as Kasravism, which strived for the fullest assimilation of the people of Iranian Azerbaijan into Iranian culture. In his writings during **World War II**, Kasravi tended to be more critical of Great Britain than of the USSR, despite the fact that the Red Army occupation authorities encouraged nationalist-autonomist movement in Iranian Azerbaijan. Kasravi was assassinated by a religious fanatic for his supposed heresy. *See also* IRANIAN AZERBAIJAN.

KAVBIURO (CAUCASIAN BUREAU OF THE CENTRAL COMMITTEE OF THE RCP[B]. A body representing the Central Committee of the Russian Communist Party (Bolshevik) in the Caucasus region. The Bureau was formed on April 8, 1920, as the supreme Bolshevik authority in the region. Its chairman was Grigorii Ordzhonikidze and Sergei M. Kirov its deputy. The Kavbiuro supervised the operation of overthrowing the **Azerbaijani Democratic Republic** in April 1920. Subsequently the Bureau consisted of two *Troikas* (Committees of Three), in **Baku** and Armavir, which were responsible for the party organizations of **Transcaucasia** and the Northern Caucasus, respectively. The Bureau was dissolved by the First Congress of the Communist Organizations of Transcaucasia in February 1922. *See also* AZERBAIJANI DEMOCRATIC REPUBLIC; AZREVKOM.

KESRANIDS. A dynasty of the state of the **Shirvanshahs** that ruled from 1027 to 1382. The Shirvanshah state controlled the territory from the **Kura River** to the town of Derbent, and had as its capital She-makha. The Kesranid dynasty grew rich on the oil and salt trades. The Shirvanshah state achieved its greatest power during the rule of Min-uchihr II (1120–1149) and Achsitan (1149–1203) when it was the cen-ter of the struggle against the Seljuks. The Kesranids were replaced by the **Derbent Shirvanshah** dynasty. *See also* DERBENT SHIRVAN-SHAHS; SHIRVAN; SHIRVANSHAHS.

KHALKALI, JAVADZADE. *See* PISHEVARI, JAFAR SAYYID.

KHIABANI, SHAIKH MUHAMMAD (1880–1920). A well educated cleric, deputy to the Iranian Majlis from **Tabriz,** and the political leader of the province of Azerbaijan. In 1917 he founded the **Democratic Party of Azerbaijan** (DPAz) over the protest of some Tabrizis, who were suspicious of his intentions to loosen ties with the central govern-ment of Iran. During the Ottoman occupation of **Iranian Azerbaijan** in the fall of 1918, Khiabani was exiled to Kars. Upon his return from exile, he declined to endorse the demands for linguistic Persianization coming from some members of the DPAz. His practice of addressing the public in Azeri paid off with the growth of his popularity and polit-ical influence in Tabriz. He led the Azerbaijani protest movement against the August 1919 agreement between Britain and the Teheran regime as harmful to the interests of Iran. On April 9, 1920, the DPAz under Khiabani staged a revolt in Tabriz against the Teheran-appointed governor, and proclaimed an autonomous region to be called **Azadis-tan** (Land of Freedom). Khiabani called for implementation of the con-stitution and local autonomy. The landing of Red Army troops at En-zeli in support of Mirza Kuchuk Khan's regime in Gīlān made him suspicious of Soviet intentions. The Tabriz revolt was crushed by Iran-ian government forces intent upon the restoration of central authority in the provinces. On September 4, 1920, Iranian Cossacks entered Tabriz, dispersed the DPAz, and killed Khiabani. *See also* AZADISTAN; DEMOCRATIC PARTY OF AZERBAIJAN (1917–1920).

KHOISKI, FATH ALI KHAN (1875–1920). By profession a lawyer, Fath Ali Khan Khoiski was a prominent political figure in Azerbaijani politics and a deputy to the Second State Duma of Russia. In the period of independence he became the first prime minister of the **Azerbaijani Democratic Republic** on May 28, 1918. As a member of the Indepen-dent group not linked to any political party, he continued as prime minister until replaced by Nasib bey **Yusufbeyli** on April 5, 1919. In December 1919 he was named minister of foreign affairs. Following the overthrow of the Democratic Republic, he headed the Committee for Salvation of Azerbaijan located in Tbilisi, where he was assassinated in 1920. *See also* AZERBAIJANI DEMOCRATIC REPUBLIC.

KHURRAMIYA SECT. An Islamic sect whose name is derived from Khurram, a district of Ardabil where the sect may have arisen. They were active in Iran, Azerbaijan, and Central Asia in the early period of Abbasid rule. Their tenets combined Mazdakism with an appeal for social reform and a belief in transmigration and the successive incarnations of the holy spirit in the personality of various prophets and *imams*. The sect took part in various uprisings such as that of Abu Muslim of 747–750, the Sumbad-mag uprising of 755, the Red Banners rebellion of 778–779, the Mukanna Uprising of the 770s and 780s, and the **Babak Uprising** of 816–837.

KIROVABAD. *See* GANJA.

KORENIZATSIIA **(NATIVIZATION).** Soviet policy adopted in 1923 as a part of a social contract with the non-Russian nationalities of the newly formed Soviet Union. Apart from securing for natives positions in the local Communist Party and government, korenizatsiia also called for full equality of national languages with Russian, and generally attempted to reconcile the nationalities to the Soviet rule.

Inasmuch as *korenizatsiia* offered the promise of overcoming backwardness and underdevelopment, it met some of the Azeri **intelligentsia**'s aspirations halfway. In the climate of nativization, its members resumed their time-honored pursuits of a **Jadidist**-enlightenment character, such as combating illiteracy, setting up new schools, promoting women's rights, expanding communication media, and developing of a literary language based on native vernacular. With the revision of Soviet nationality policies and official promotion of Russian language and civilization in the late 1920s, *korenizatsiia* ceased to be regarded as an absolute value in itself, and its application was drastically reduced. *See also* ALPHABET REFORM; EDUCATION; INTELLIGENTSIA.

KRAIKOM (REGIONAL COMMITTEE OF THE RCP[B]). The highest Bolshevik authority south of the **Caucasus Mountains** during the period of the Russian Revolution and the early 1920s. The Kraikom was based in Georgia's capital, Tbilisi.

KUBA KHANATE. A principality in Azerbaijan that arose following the assassination of the Iranian ruler **Nadir Shah** in 1747. It was centered on the city of Kuba. From 1758 to 1789 it was headed by **Fath Ali Khan,** who united and controlled all of the Caspian lands of Azerbaijan as far as Ardabil in the south. However, in 1784 Russia forced him to relinquish most of his conquests. Following Fath Ali Khan's death in 1789, the khanate fell into decline and was occupied by Russian troops, who put down an uprising there in 1806. Russian hegemony over the khanate was confirmed by the Treaty of **Gulistan** in 1813. In the 1820s Russian military authorities abolished the Kuba Khanate. *See also* FATH ALI KHAN OF KUBA.

KURA RIVER. Flowing through Georgia, Azerbaijan, and Turkey, the Kura River rises in the Armenian Highlands in Turkey and empties into the **Caspian Sea.** It is 846 miles (1,364 km) long. In its upper reaches, as far as Tbilisi, it flows mainly through ravines and gorges alternating with basins and plains. Below Tbilisi the river flows between the Borchala Plain and the arid Karaiazskaia Steppe. It receives water from its tributary the Alazani River before flowing into the Mingechaur Reservoir. Below Mingechaur the Kura meanders through the Kura-Araxes lowland before being joined by the waters of the **Araxes River.** At the point where it enters the Caspian Sea, the Kura forms a delta covering an area of 39 square miles (100 sq km). Along the Kura are situated the towns of Borzhomi, Gori, Mtskheta, Tbilisi, Rustavi, Mingechaur, Evlakh, Sabirabad, Ali-Bairamly, and Sal'yany.

-L-

LANGUAGE, AZERI. The language of the Azeris is close to modern Turkish and belongs to the southwest group of the Turkic division of the Ural-Altaic language family. It derives from the language of the **Oghuz** tribes of Central Asia from the seventh to 11th centuries. The Azeri language has four closely related dialect groups, each with a number of subdialects: eastern (including **Kuba, Baku,** and Shemakha dialects), western (including Kazak, **Ganja, Karabagh,** and Airum dialects), northern (including Nukha and Zakataly-Kazak dialects), and southern (including **Nakhichevan** and **Erivan,** and the dialects spoken in Iran). Azeri literature began to appear in the 11th century. The Baku dialect forms the basis of the modern Azeri literary language. The language was written in the Arabic script until 1923, the Latin alphabet from 1924 to 1940, and the modified Russian Cyrillic alphabet since 1940. Since independence from the Soviet Union on August 30, 1991, there has been a return to the Latin alphabet. *See also* ALPHABET REFORM.

LESGINS. An ethno-linguistic Caucasian group inhabiting the borderland of **Daghestan** and Azerbaijan. There are 205,000 Lesgins in Daghestan and 180,000 in Azerbaijan. They were first divided by the tsarist regime in 1861 between the provinces of Baku and Daghestan, and then again by Stalin in 1920 between the Azerbaijani SSR and the Daghestan ASSR. With the demise of the Soviet Union, the Lesgin problem became a factor in relations between Russia and the independent **Republic of Azerbaijan.** In 1990, the emerging Lesgin national movement, *Sadval,* raised the demand for a unified autonomous republic, Lesgistan, and in March 1993 bloody clashes between police and secessionist demonstrators occurred in the Azerbaijani town of Kusary. Moscow used the Lesgin problem as a means to exert pressure on **Baku** during **Elchibey's** presidency. It offered support to a Lesgin political front, and withdrew it abruptly upon **Aliyev**'s return to power. *See also* DAGHESTAN.

LITERATURE, AZERI. In folklore, classical Islamic poetry, and modern literary forms, it offers one of the finest examples of the creativity of the Turkic peoples. The oldest form is the *dastan,* an epic story, sometimes recited to music, which combines historical themes and traditions with poetry. In Azerbaijan the *dastans* have been the major source for ethnic identity, custom, and community values. Of the *dastans,* the oldest and most important are *The Book of Dede Korkut* and *Koroghlu,* which date, in written form, from the 15th century.

   Early Azeri poetry is a mixture of Iranian and Turkic cultural roots. Prominent among the poets revered by Azeris are: **Nizami** Ganjevi (1141–1209), whose *Khamseh* contains five epic poems that are based on traditional stories; **Fuzuli** (1494–1556), who wrote his lyrical poerty in Azeri; Shah **Ismail** Safavid (1486–1524), who wrote Azeri poetry under the pseudonym Khatai. These are part of the literary heritage shared with the Turks of Anatolia. A special trait of Azeri literature has been the oral poetry of the *ashugs,* folk troubadours whose tradition survives to the present.

Modern literature emerged within a generation following the completion of the conquest by Russia. Its rise was symbolized by the towering literary figure, Mirza Fath Ali **Akhundzade** (1812–1878). A defining characteristic of modern literature is a concern with popularizing the ideas of European-style enlightenment, rationalism, and education. This concern in turn promoted the growing use of spoken Azeri as the literary **language,** which gradually replaced Persian as the written idiom. Along with European ideas came new literary forms. Drama was introduced by Akhundzade and was further developed by Najaf bey **Vazirov** (1854–1926) and Abdurrahman Haqverdiyev (1870–1933). Press publishing was started in 1875 by Hasan bey **Zardabi** (1932–1907) with his newspaper *Akinchi* (Ploughman). Modern Azeri literature showed an inclination toward secularism which was seen as a means of blunting the Shi'ite-Sunni sectarian antagonism, the condition that delayed building a cohesive community.

A powerful stimulus for Azeri literature was the impact of the "age of three revolutions," which began with the Russian Revolution of 1905, and covered the **Iranian Constitutional Revolution** of 1906–1911, and the **Young Turkish Revolution** of 1908 in the Ottoman Empire. The hopes awakened by this period of revolutionary upheavals found their artistic expression in the poetry of Alakpar **Sabir** (1862–1911). Among other leading writers of this time were Jalil Mammad **Quluzade** (1866–1932), who published the famous literary-satirical magazine, *Molla Nasr al-din;* the playwright **Huseyn Javid;** and the poet Mammad Hadi. The latter two represented a new trend, romanticism. The post-1905 literary revival put into focus the issue of purification of the language, this time from Ottoman Turkish influences that were creeping in along with the idea of **Pan-Turkism** and the unity of Turkic peoples. The most eloquent spokesman for Pan-Turkism was Ali bey **Huseynzade** and his literary review, *Fuyuzat* (Abundance).

The Soviet period brought an expansion of the reading public, a result of the decreasing illiteracy ratio, especially after the latinization of the alphabet. Yet, in the 1930s the Union of Azerbaijani Writers became a special target of Stalin's purges. Among the victims were the leading literary figures of the country, such as Huseyn Javid, Salman Mumtaz, Qurban Musayev, Taqi Shahbazi, Ali Nazim, and Mikail Mushfiq. Socialist Realism was imposed as the norm, and strict political conformism led to a general decline in artistic qualities, despite the evidence of genuine literary talents in some writers. Among these stood out Samad Vurgun, Jafar Jabbarli, and Ilyas Effendiyev.

In the years following **World War II,** a literary trend of special significance was the "literature of longing," which centered on the theme of the closeness of Soviet and **Iranian Azerbaijan.** Its most outstanding representatives were the novelists Mammad Said Ordubadi (1872–1950) and Mirza Ibrahimov (b. 1911), and the poets Suleiman Rustamov and Bakhtiar Vahabzade. A new period followed with the advent of *glasnost* in the late 1980s. One of its earliest manifestations was the rehabilitation of formerly banned writers and their works. A proliferation of newspapers, literary magazines, and works by young authors was also a part of the impressive intellectual revival stimulated as much by *glasnost* as by the increasing contacts with the outside, non-Soviet world. *See also* DEDE KORKUT, THE BOOK OF; PRESS; THEATER, AZERI.

LOWER CAUCASUS RANGE. The Lower Caucasus Range forms the southern border of **Transcaucasia.** It winds through the **Nakhichevan** Autonomous Republic, Armenia, the **Nagorno-Karabagh** region, and Azerbaijan and stretches along the **Araxes River** to the **Caspian Sea.**

-M-

MAMMADQULUZADE, JALIL. *See* QULUZADE MAMMAD JALIL.

MANNAI. An ancient state of the first millennium B.C. located in **Transcaucasia.** It is first mentioned in historical sources in 843 B.C. and was located in the basin of the Jhagatu River. Its capital was the city of Izirtu (Zirta). Mannai became a large state by incorporating the neighboring regions occupied by the Hurrians, Lullubi, Guti, and Kassites.

The power of Mannai was strengthened after the victory of its ally, Assyria, over Urartu in 715–714 B.C. In 660–659 B.C. Mannai was conquered by Assyria. Mannai remained an Assyrian dependency until Assyria's defeat by the neo-Babylonian Empire and Media in 616 B.C. By 590 B.C. Mannai was incorporated into the Median empire. *See also* MEDIA.

MARCH DAYS OF 1918. A series of violent events that resulted in a temporary seizure of power by the Bolsheviks in **Baku** in 1918. The roots of the violence reached back to the tensions between the Muslim and Armenian communities in the city. The crisis began on March 24, when the Baku Soviet ordered the disarming of the men from the Muslim "Savage Division" of the Russian army arriving in Baku. This action outraged the Baku Muslims who were alarmed that their military unit would be disarmed while the Armenian and Russian communities kept large, well-armed forces. At night barricades were erected, and talks between Muslim representatives and the Baku Soviet broke down. When an armed confrontation began, the Dashnakist forces, which had at first declared their neutrality, joined the side of the Soviets. Even after the **Azeri** leaders accepted the authority of the Soviets over Baku, the Dashnakists, among whom were numerous refugees from Turkey, staged the massacre of the city's Muslims. The debacle lasted from March 31 to April 2, and resulted in at least 3,000 fatalities, many of them immigrants from Iran. Thousands of Azeri survivors fled the city in panic. With their political organizations disbanded, their leaders sought refuge in **Ganja** or Tbilisi.

After suppressing potential opposition, a new executive body, the Baku Soviet of People's Commissars (Sovnarkom) was proclaimed on April 25 as the local replica of Lenin's government. The March Days alienated most of the Azeris from the Bolsheviks, and the establishment of Soviet power over the city was seen as Russian-Armenian rule at the expense of the Muslims. *See also* ARMENIANS; BAKU COMMUNE.

MAZYADIDS. A dynasty of the **Shirvanshah** state that ruled over northern Azerbaijan from the ninth to the early 11th century. The Shirvanshah state controlled the territory from the **Kura River** to the town of Derbent, and had its capital at the city of Shemakha. The Mazyadids were replaced as the rulers of **Shirvan** by the **Kesranids**. *See also* KESRANIDS; SHIRVAN; SHIRVANSHAHS.

MEDIA. An ancient kingdom located in the northwestern part of the Iranian Plateau. The first historical references to the Medes, who inhabited this region, come from Assyrian annals of the ninth century B.C. The kingdom of Media arose in the 670s B.C. and became a great power in the region, conquering the **Mannai** state and, in alliance with Babylonia, crushed the Assyrian Empire and Urartu. In 550 B.C. Media was conquered by the Achaemenid Empire of Iran and made a satrapy. An independent Median state was restored in the fourth century B.C., but only occupied southern Azerbaijan, which came to be called Median Atropatene. The area was subsequently conquered by one of Alexander the Great's generals and later became a part of the Seleucid Empire. *See also* MANNAI.

MILLI MAJLIS. *See* NATIONAL COUNCIL.

MINGECHAUR RESERVOIR. A reservoir created to facilitate agriculture, water transportation, and the production of electrical power. In addition, it was designed to eliminate flooding in the lower course of the **Kura River.** The filling of the reservoir began in 1953 and was completed in 1959. It has an area of 234 square miles (605 sq km), a length of 44 miles (70 km), a width of 11 miles (18 km), and an average depth of 89 feet (27 m).

MOLLA NASR AL-DIN. A literary-satirical magazine founded in 1906 in Tbilisi by Jalil Mammad **Quluzade.** The most widely circulated press publication in Azeri, *Molla Nasr al-din* commented on contemporary issues of the period of revolutions in Russia, Iran, and Turkey. It gained popularity in the neighboring Muslim countries, especially in Iran and **Iranian Azerbaijan** where it influenced the growth of the local press. Among its subscribers were illiterates who enjoyed the magazine's famous cartoons. *Molla Nasr al-din* was firmly opposed to the trend toward the Ottomanization of the literary **language,** and was an outspoken champion of using Azeri as the literary language of the country. *See also* AZARIJILAR; LITERATURE; QULUZADE, MAMMAD JALIL.

MUHAJIRIN (IMMIGRANTS). A term applied to persons arriving in **Iranian Azerbaijan** from the Soviet Union in the mid-1930s. The Muhajirin were often Iranian citizens who had settled in Soviet Azerbaijan and been expelled during the Great Purges of the 1930s. The Iranian authorities looked upon them as being contaminated by communism and did not assist in their integration into local communities. On their part, the Muhajirin tended to regard the USSR as a land of greater opportunity, and they formed a pool of pro-Soviet sympathies in Iranian Azerbaijan. Under the **Autonomous Government of Azerbaijan,** they were a source of support for the regime and provided political officers for the Azerbaijani Army. Following that government's demise, many Muhajirin fled to the USSR. *See also* AUTONOMOUS GOVERNMENT OF AZERBAIJAN; IRANIAN AZERBAIJAN.

MUSAFARID DYNASTY. Also known as Sallarids or Kangarids. A dynasty of Iranian origin that ruled Azerbaijan in the second half of the 10th century. The dynasty was founded by Muhammad Musafir about 916. Originally rulers of Daylam, the Musafir family split after 941, with Wahsudan remaining ruler of Daylam while his brother Marzuban seized Azerbaijan, **Arran,** and **Derbent.**

In 971 the Shaddadids drove the Musafarids from Arran, and Ibrahim Musafarid was defeated by the Rawwadids in 981. As a consequence of this defeat the **Rawwadid dynasty** replaced the Musafarids as the rulers of Azerbaijan. The Musafarid dynasty's fortunes revived briefly after that and they were able to occupy Zanjān and other towns to the south of Daylam. But in 1029 they were driven out of Tarom by the Ghaznavids and later became vassals of the **Seljuk** Turks. It is probable that the last Musafarids were extinguished by the Ismailis of Alamut. *See also* RAWWADI DYNASTY.

MUSAVAT (EQUALITY) PARTY. The most continuous Azerbaijani political party, holding at times a central position in the nation's politics. The Musavat was founded in **Baku** in October 1911 by former members of the Social-Democratic **Himmat** Party. The founders, among whom were Karbalai Mikailzade, Abbas Kazimzade, and Qulam Rza Sharifzade, shared a disillusionment with the Russian Revolution and an awareness of the worldwide stirring among Islamic peoples.

Musavat's first program of political action called for the unity of all Muslims regardless of nationality or sectarian affiliation, restoration of the lost independence of Muslim countries, and assistance to Muslim peoples struggling for the preservation of their independence. The program was notable for its generalities, and it clearly intended to accommodate a broad spectrum of the public. The largest part of the Musavat's following came from the ranks of the **intelligentsia,** students, entrepreneurs, and merchants. Its geographical base of support was the metropolitan area of Baku. For reasons of security, the members were organized into three-person cells, and the concealment proved to be so effective that the Musavat did not give many signs of life until the overthrow of Tsar Nicholas II in March 1917.

In the new era of freedom, the Musavat became the largest political force in Azerbaijan. A different party from the handful of former Himmatists of the pre-war years, the new **Musavat** evolved from the merger of the old Baku-based cadre with the **Ganja** Turkic Party of Federalists, which traced its roots to the **Difai.** The group's full name, reflecting its hybrid character, was the Turkic Party of Federalists—Musavat. In effect, the Musavat consisted of two distinct wings, the Left, or Baku wing, led by Mammad Amin **Rasulzade** and Mammad Hasan **Hajinski,** and the Right, or **Ganja** wing, led by Nasib bey **Yusufbeyli,** Hasan Aghazade, Shafi Rustambekov, and the brothers Alakpar and Khalil Khasmammadov. The wings differed on social and economic issues, most notably that of land reform, but were held together by two overriding commitments. One was secular Turkic nationalism, the other was the vision of Azerbaijan as an autonomous republic in association with a Russia restructured into a federation of free and equal republics.

The program of federalism adopted in October 1917 marked a new stage of Azerbaijan's evolution: the transition toward a nation-state. The Musavat's impulse to federalize was to remain a constant rather than transitory trait, rooted as it was in doubts about the viability of a fully independent Azerbaijan.

In the period of the independent Democratic Republic, the Musavat continued as the largest political force in Azerbaijan, but it held only 38 seats in the 96-man Parliament, and the formation of a government was possible only with the participation of other parties. Of the five cabinets in the period of independence, the last two were headed by Yusufbeyli (April 4, 1919; December 29, 1919). According to the declaration of Rasulzade in the Parliament, the Musavat party in the era of democracy was to be guided by the principals of nationalism and federalism. The meaning of nationalism was now embodied in the recognition that the **Azeris,** while part of a larger family of Turkic peoples, constituted a nation of their own. As for the second principle, the question with whom to federalize was left open. Later, in post-independence years, the Musavat would be criticized for its implicit readiness to federalize with diverse partners—not only their Transcaucasian neighbors, Georgia and Armenia, but also Iran, Turkey, and Russia, White or Red.

In the face of the impending invasion of Azerbaijan by the Red Army in the spring of 1920, cracks appeared in the Musavat unity, and the Left wing led by Hajinski, with support of Rasulzade, took a more accommodating position toward the coming of Soviet power. Under the Soviet regime, the Musavat was allowed to exist in the form of its Left wing, to the exclusion of the Rightists whose surviving leaders resided abroad. In 1923, the Musavatists, after growing harassment by the Cheka, found themselves under pressure to dissolve the party altogether on the grounds that its work had become superfluous after the recently proclaimed Soviet nationality program. The legal existence of the Musavat in Azerbaijan ended on August 14, 1923. During the 1920s some party cells remained active underground in Azerbaijan, a crime under the Soviet law for which the Musavatists were severely punished. In the mid-1920s the members of the Musavat formed the largest contingent of the inmates in the Solovki Island prison camp. Otherwise, the party continued in exile, mainly in Turkey and Iran, as the main force in émigré politics under the umbrella of the Azerbaijani National Center.

Despite frequent squabbles, the Musavatists actively supported the initiatives to revive the programs of Transcaucasian or Caucasian federalism. In 1928 the rebellion against the leadership of Rasulzade resulted in the secession from the party of a group of rightists headed by Rustambekov and Khasmammadov.

The Musavat joined the Promethean Movement devoted to liberation of non-Russian nationalities of the USSR, and after 1930 Rasulzade moved the party's center from Turkey to Poland.

With Polish assistance the Brussels Pact was hammered out providing for a confederate rather than a federal structure of the Caucasian state of the future. The pact received endorsement from the Azerbaijani, Georgian, and Caucasian Mountaineer émigré centers, leaving the door open for Armenian participation. The spirit of the Brussels Pact together with the leadership of Rasulzade found confirmation within the party from the clandestine congress of the Musavat that met in Warsaw in 1936.

At the outbreak of **World War II,** the number of active members of the Musavat in Turkey and Iran was estimated at no more than 150. In Soviet Azerbaijan, the party's potential influence was seen as extensive, although in hibernation. As a party, the Musavat showed steadily decreasing signs of life during the war and post-war period.

With the collapse of the Soviet regime, the party was revived under the name Yeni Musavat (New Musavat), which was subsequently changed to simply Musavat. Led by Isa Gambar, the party has, from 1993 on, remains in opposition to the regime of Haidar **Aliyev.** It was banned from taking part in the 1995 parliamentary elections. *See also* AZERBAIJANI DEMOCRATIC REPUBLIC; RASULZADE, MAMMAD AMIN.

MUSLIM NATIONAL CORPS. A military unit that was formed following the overthrow of Tsar Nicholas II in March 1917. The corps was to redress the imbalance in military training between the Muslims of **Transcaucasia** and their Christian neighbors due to the tsarist policy of exempting Muslims from the draft. The **Azeri** disadvantage against the militarily well-trained **Armenians** alarmed leaders of the **Musavat,** in view of growing intercommunal tensions. Despite intense lobbying, the provisional government of Russia under Alexander Kerenskii withheld its assent to the forming of the Muslim National Corps until the end of September 1917. The corps did not begin forming until after the fall of the provisional government in October 1917, with the cavalry regiment of the Savage Division, transferred from Petrograd, as its nucleus. General Ali Agha Shikhlinski assumed command of the corps and drew officers from the ranks of the tsarist army. To avoid an overreliance on Christian officers from the Imperial Army, preference in recruitment was given to Muslims, and training of native officers began in **Baku**. To obtain sufficient arms the Azeris began disarming Russian troops, which led to incidents such as the **Shamkhor Massacre**. With arms in their possession, the corps began taking over the countryside and clashing with Armenians.

In 1918 the Muslim National Corps joined the Ottoman Fifth Infantry Division and bands of irregulars to form the **Army of Islam.** This unit was disbanded following the Ottoman defeat in October 1918, and much of it became part of the army of the Azerbaijani Democratic Republic. *See also* ARMY OF ISLAM; SHAMKHOR MASSACRE.

MUSLIM SOCIALIST BLOC. The **Azeri** equivalent of the Russian Social Revolutionaries, which emerged in the fall of 1917. The group was led by Aslan bey Safikiurdski and Ibrahim Haidarov and sought the support of the peasantry. In November 1917 the Muslim Socialist Bloc won two seats in the elections to the Russian Constituent Assembly. Its representation was proportionately increased in the **Transcaucasian Seim**. Following the proclamation of independence in May 1918, the deputies of the bloc withdrew from the National Council in protest to Ottoman meddling in Azerbaijani internal affairs. Haidarov was dropped from the new cabinet that was formed on June 17th since it was believed that he was too far to the left. The bloc resumed full participation in Azerbaijan's political life until the invasion of the Red Army in April 1920. *See also* AZERBAIJANI DEMOCRATIC REPUBLIC.

MUSLIM SOCIALIST BUREAU. A coordinating body of left-wing Muslim organizations formed in **Baku** in 1918. The bureau included representatives of the **Himmat, Adalat,** and **Akinchi** parties. It was recognized by the Baku Sovnarkom as the sole voice of the Muslims under the **Baku Commune,** the regime that emerged after the fighting between **Azeris** and **Armenians** known as the **March Days of 1918.** The bureau sought to protect the welfare and security of the Muslim community of Baku against violence on the part of the Armenians.

MUSTAFAYEV, IMAM DASHDEMIROGHLU (b. 1910). A scientist with little experience in party work, Mustafayev was elevated to the position of the leadership of the **Communist Party of Azerbaijan** (CPAz) in 1954, replacing Mir Jafar **Baghirov.** In his post as first secretary, Mustafayev attempted to restore some of Azerbaijan's autonomy by maintaining the country's oil ministry separate from the Soviet Union's central control. Moreover, he resisted implementation of the legislation giving the Russian language precedence over the native language in Azerbaijan. In June 1959, he was ousted from the office on the grounds of "having caused bewilderment in the completely clear language question." His replacement as first secretary of the CPAz was Veli **Akhundov.**

MUTALIBOV, AYAZ NIYAZI OGHLI (1938–   ). The last head of the **Communist Party of Azerbaijan,** and the first president of the post-Soviet Azerbaijani Republic. He succeeded Abdul Rakhman **Vazirov** as first secretary of the CPAz after the 1990 ethnic violence in **Baku** known as **Black January.** His image was tarnished by his expressed support for the plotters of the August 1991 coup attempt against Mikhail Gorbachev, provoking calls for his resignation. Instead, Mutalibov ran unopposed in the presidential elections of the newly proclaimed Azerbaijani Republic.

As the president, he was increasingly criticized for his failure to build up the national army, which was needed to stem the Armenian advances into Azerbaijani territory in the **Nagorno-Karabagh dispute.** In an act that marked the political ascendance of the opposition **People's Front of Azerbaijan,** the Parliament forced Mutalibov to resign in March 1992. After a brief and abortive attempt at recovering his power in May 1992, he went into exile in Russia. *See also* NAGORNO-KARABAGH DISPUTE; REPUBLIC OF AZERBAIJAN.

-N-

NADIR SHAH AFSHAR (1688–1747). Born in Khurasan, Nadir Shah entered the service of Shah Tahmasp II in 1726. As Tahmasp's general he conducted successful campaigns against Ottoman and Afghani encroachment on Iranian territory. As a popular figure Nadir enjoyed the support necessary to topple Tahmasp from the Iranian throne in 1732 and proclaim Tahmasp's son (Shah Abbas III) ruler, with himself as regent. In 1736 he proclaimed himself the shah.

Nadir Shah centralized power in his own hands and embarked on wars of conquest. His large empire consisted of Iran, Armenia, Azerbaijan, Georgia, **Daghestan,** Afghanistan, Baluchistan, and the Khiva and Bukhara khanates. He campaigned in northern India from 1737 to 1739, capturing Delhi. The harsh rule and high taxes he imposed to finance his wars sparked numerous revolts within his empire. On June 20, 1747, Nadir Shah was murdered in Khubushan by one of the factions at his court. His death started a long period of government disintegration in Iran, making possible the rise of independent, or virtually so, Azerbaijani khanates.

NAGORNO-KARABAGH. Historically, a mountainous part of the **Karabagh Khanate,** under the Soviet rule of an **Armenian** enclave, with the status of an autonomous Oblast (district) within Azerbaijan. With its slopes, rivers, and valleys, Nagorno-Karabagh is open toward the east, in the general direction of the **Caspian** coast, rather than toward Armenia, from which it is separated by a mountain barrier. The *oblast* territory covers 1,700 square miles (4,403 sq km), its population in 1989 was 192,000, and its capital is Xankändi (Stepanakert).

The chief industries of Nagorno-Karabagh are silk, wine, dairy farming, and building materials. Its chief agricultural products are cotton, grapes, and winter wheat. Before the Russian conquest Nagorno-Karabagh was an Armenian-populated part of the **Karabagh Khanate,** under the authority of the local *meliks* (rulers). Included under the tsardom the Elizavetpol *guberniia,* Nagorno-Karabagh formed a part of a geographic and economic entity of **Eastern Transcaucasia,** the core of which would one day be independent Azerbaijan. After the Soviet conquest, Nagorno-Karabagh was established as an autonomous district within the Azerbaijani SSR (Nagorno-Karabagh Autonomous Oblast) in 1923.

In December 1991, after almost three years of interethnic violence, Nagorno-Karabagh declared its independence from Azerbaijan and asked for admission into the Commonwealth of Independent States. Azerbaijan responded by abolishing the autonomous status of Nagorno-Karabagh. The unresolved military conflict resulted in Armenian control over the oblast and forcible deportation of the local **Azeri** minority. *See also* NAGORNO-KARABAGH DISPUTE.

NAGORNO-KARABAGH DISPUTE. The most violent and protracted territorial and ethnic conflict that followed the demise of the Soviet Union. Historically, this mountainous part of the **Karabagh Khanate** was an arena of tensions between the sedentary, **Armenian,** and pastoral Muslim population competing for grazing grounds. At the end of the Russian conquest of Azerbaijan in the 1830s, estimates of the Armenian population of Karabagh were 19,000 against 34,000 Muslims, with the Armenians concentrated in the mountainous part of the khanate. During the 1905–1907 Revolution, Nagorno-Karabagh, and especially the region's main town, Shusha, became one of the centers of Muslim-Armenian violence. The violence reemerged in the period of independence, but in 1919 the local Armenian assembly formally accepted Azerbaijani rule in recognition of the realities of geography, economy, and transportation that linked this ethnic enclave with Azerbaijan rather than with Armenia beyond the mountain barrier. The settlement proved to be short-lived as in March 1920 an Armenian uprising broke out in Nagorno-Karabagh on the eve of the Red Army's invasion of Azerbaijan.

With the coming of Soviet power the Nagorno-Karabagh problem appeared more intractable than before. The new regime in **Baku** at first insisted on the withdrawal of Armenian forces from Nagorno-Karabagh and Zangezur. Then, in December 1920, Nariman **Narimanov** declared that the disputed region would be ceded to Armenia, which was about to be Sovietized. It took almost three years of complex maneuvering, with the participation of Stalin, before a compromise between the economic integration of Nagorno Karabagh with Azerbaijan and the Armenian composition of its population was found: on July 7, 1923, Nagorno-Karabagh was given the status of an Autonomous *Oblast* (district) within the Soviet Republic of Azerbaijan.

Beginning with the 1960s, Armenians were petitioning Moscow for unification of Nagorno-Karabagh with Armenia. They argued that Azerbaijan discriminated against Armenians living in the *oblast* and that Nagorno-Karabagh was economically neglected by Baku. The Azerbaijani counterclaim was that Armenians discriminated against the **Azeri** minority within Nagorno-Karabagh and that the district received more funding than larger and more populous **Nakhichevan**. In February 1988, petitioning activity gave way to mass demonstrations in Armenian cities and was followed by anti-Armenian riots in Sumgait that left 32 dead. By the end of 1988 the violence on both sides had claimed 80 lives and created 250,000 Armenian and Azeri refugees. During **Black January 1990,** the attempts at detaching Nagorno-Karabagh from Azerbaijan led to anti-Armenian riots in Baku which, in turn, brought Soviet military intervention to restore order at the cost of additional dead and wounded among the Azeris.

Within several weeks of the declaration of independence, the Azerbaijani parliament annulled the autonomous status of Nagorno-Karabagh. In a countermove, the *oblast* legislature proclaimed the independence of Nagorno-Karabagh on January 6, 1992. This act failed to gain recognition from any government, including that of the republic of Armenia. The Erivan regime gave its support to the Armenian forces fighting successful campaigns in Nagorno-Karabagh. In February 1992 Armenians seized Shusha and Lachin, a feat that opened the strategically crucial road link with Armenia around the mountain barrier. In the course of this offensive, the massacre of the Azeri population in the town of Khojaly took place. The shock over the mass murder as well as the public's indignation at the poor performance of the Azerbaijani army, forced president Ayaz **Mutalibov** to resign from office in March 1992. Under his successor, Abulfaz **Elchibey,** the Azerbaijani side continued to suffer reverses, and lost about 20 percent of the republic's territory, with the number of war refugees estimated at close to a million. The political fallout of these reverses was the overthrow of Elchibey's presidency by a military coup in June 1993.

The protracted conflict found no solution under the presidency of Haidar **Aliyev,** although both sides concluded the cease-fire agreement in effect since May 1994. Permanent peace arrangements have been negotiated under the auspices of the Minsk Group of the Commission on Security and Cooperation in Europe (OSCE). The proposals for a solution providing for the return of Nagorno-Karabagh to Azerbaijani sovereignty, which the Armenian president Levon Ter-Petrosyan was willing to accept as the basis for negotiations, led to a constitutional coup of early 1998. Ter-Petrosyan was replaced by the perceived hard-liner Robert Kochariyan. In November 1998 the

OSCE presented new proposals for a "common state" of Azerbaijan and Nagorno-Karabagh. The proposals were rejected by Baku with comments on Russian scheming. The continuing heavy supplies of arms by Russia to Armenia, including the delivery of advanced MIG 29 planes and S-300 rockets, provoked from the Azerbaijani side statements threatening the possibility of American and Turkish air forces setting up bases in Azerbaijani territory. *See also* ARMENI-ANS IN AZERBAIJAN; KARABAGH KHANATE; REPUBLIC OF AZERBAIJAN.

NAKHICHEVAN. Capital city of the Nakhichevan autonomous region within Azerbaijan. Its 1993 population was 60,000. The city was founded in the fifth century B.C. and was a large trading center as early as the eighth to 10th centuries. In the 11th century it was the residence of the **Seljuk** sultan, and in the 12th century the capital of the **Ildiguzid** dynasty. It has been pillaged by several conquerors: Mongols (13th century), Tamerlane (late 14th century), and finally the Iranians (early 17th century). During the 19th century the city was the center of the **Nakhichevan Khanate** until it was seized by Russian troops during the **Russo-Iranian War of 1826–1828**. In 1849 it became the administrative center of the Nakhichevan District of Erivan Province. In the period of the Russian Civil War, the city was occupied first by the Turkish army, then by the British, and finally by the Bolsheviks on July 28, 1920. On February 9, 1924 it became the capital of the **Nakhichevan Autonomous Soviet Socialist Republic**. Today Nakhichevan is a part of the **Republic of Azerbaijan**. *See also* NAKHICHEVAN; NAKHICHEVAN AUTONOMOUS SOVIET SOCIALIST REPUB-LIC; NAKHICHEVAN KHANATE.

NAKHICHEVAN AUTONOMOUS SOVIET SOCIALIST RE-PUBLIC. Formed on February 9, 1924, its capital is the city of **Nakhichevan**. Although part of Azerbaijan, Nakhichevan is geo-graphically separated from the rest of Azerbaijan by a 25–30 mile-wide-strip of Armenian territory (**Zangezur**) on its northeast border. To the south Nakhichevan borders Turkey and Iran. A December 1920 agreement between the Azerbaijani Soviet government and Armenia placed Nakhichevan under Armenian authority. In March 1921, in signing the Treaty of Friendship with Kemalist Turkey, Soviet Russia acceded to Turkish wishes to have a common frontier with Azerbaijan, and Nakhichevan was made part of Soviet Azerbaijan. After the creation of the USSR in 1922, Nakhichevan received the status of an Autonomous Soviet Republic, a part of the **Azerbaijani Soviet Socialist Republic**. With the passage of time, Nakhichevan lost most of its Armenian population through emigration.

Under the post-Soviet constitution of 1995, the status of Nakhichevan was redefined as an Autonomous State within the Azerbaijani Republic. *See also* NAKHICHEVAN; ZANGEZUR.

NAKHICHEVAN KHANATE. An Azerbaijani principality created in 1747 after the assassination of **Nadir Shah** of Iran. At the close of the **Russo-Iranian War** of 1826–1828, the khanate was absorbed by Russia in accordance with the Treaty of **Turkmanchai** of 1828. *See also* NAKHICHEVAN.

NARIMANOV, NARIMAN NAJAFOGHLI (1870–1925). A leading figure in Azerbaijani left-wing politics in the age of revolution. Born on April 2, 1870, in Tbilisi, Narimanov graduated from Gori Teacher's Seminary in 1890 and from the medical faculty of Novorossiysk University in 1908 as the recipient of a grant from Zaynal Abdin **Taghiyev**. A man of diverse talents, he was also a writer, journalist, playwright, and educator. As a member of the Russian Social-Democratic Workers Party (RSDWP), he joined the Muslim Socialist group **Himmat** in 1905. The next year, he organized the association of Iranian immigrant workers, **Ijtima-i Amiyyun** (Social Democracy). He was arrested in 1909 and exiled to Astrakhan.

He returned to **Baku** in 1913 and worked within the ranks of the RSDWP. In 1917, he became the head of the Bolshevik wing of the restored **Himmat Party**. After the fall of the **Baku Commune** he took refuge in Russia where he spent Azerbaijan's period of independence. He held high positions in the Soviet Commissariat of Foreign Affairs and then the Commissariat of Nationalities Affairs. Here he worked closely with Joseph Stalin and gained influence in shaping Soviet policy toward Muslims. With the invasion of the Red Army, Narimanov returned to Azerbaijan and became the head of the Azerbaijani Sovnarkom. He was an advocate of Soviet Russia's assistance to revolutionary-national movements in the neighboring Muslim countries and objected to the withdrawal of this aid from the Iranian revolutionary Mirza Kuchuk Khan. His disagreements with the **Kavbiuro,** as well as the younger generation of communist **Azeri** leaders, gained him a transfer from Azerbaijan to Moscow in 1923, where he assumed the largely ceremonial position of one of the four chairs of the Central Executive Committee of the USSR. He died in his glorified exile in Moscow in 1925.

His memory became the target of special vilification in the 1930s by the head of the **Communist Party of Azerbaijan,** Mir Jafar **Baghirov.** He first castigated Narimanov as a "bourgeois nationalist," "deviationist," and "deserter" and subsequently ordered that his name remain unmentionable in any context. Only under the post-Stalin "thaw" would Narimanov's memory be exonerated, and then elevated to the symbolic father-figure of the Soviet Azerbaijani nation. *See also* HIMMAT PARTY; COMMUNIST PARTY OF AZERBAIJAN.

NATIONAL CHARTER (MISAK-I MILLI). After constituting itself into the **Azerbaijan National Council** on May 28, 1918, the Council proclaimed the independence of Azerbaijan. The independence proclamation later referred to as the National Charter reads as follows:

1. Azerbaijan is a fully sovereign state; it consists of the southern and eastern parts of Transcaucasia under the authority of the Azeri people.
2. It is resolved that the form of government of the independent Azerbaijani state is a democratic republic.
3. The Azerbaijani Democratic Republic is determined to establish friendly relations with all, especially with the neighboring nations and states.
4. The Azerbaijani Democratic Republic guarantees to all its citizens within its borders full civil and political rights, regardless of ethnic origin, religion, class, profession, or sex.
5. The Azerbaijani Democratic Republic encourages the free development of all nationalities inhabiting its territory.
6. Until the Azerbaijani Constituent Assembly is convened, the supreme authority over Azerbaijan is vested in a universally elected National Council and the provisional government responsible to the Council.

See also AZERBAIJANI DEMOCRATIC REPUBLIC.

NATIONAL COUNCIL (MILLI MAJLIS). In tacit recognition of the Supreme Soviet's doubtful legitimacy after the 1990 elections, the regime of President **Mutalibov** agreed to the formation in late November 1991 of an extraordinary legislative body. The 50-person National

Council gave equal representation to the former Communist power elite and the opposition. It overshadowed the Supreme Soviet of the **Azerbaijani Soviet Socialist Republic** as the focus of power in the independent state, although the Soviet continued its existence. After an unsuccessful attempt at recovering power by the former president Mutalibov, the Supreme Soviet dissolved itself on May 14, 1992, transferring all of its powers to the National Council. *See also* REPUBLIC OF AZERBAIJAN.

NIZAMI GANJEVI, ABU MUHAMMAD ILYAS IBN YUSUF (1141–1209). One of Iran's greatest poets. Born in the town of **Ganja,** Nizami wrote in Persian and his long literary works are famous throughout southwestern Asia. In 1173 he married a Turkish slave girl, Afaq, whom he glorified in his verse. His best-known work is the *Khamseh* (The Quintuplet), a collection of five romantic epic poems: *The Treasury of Mysteries, Khusrow and Shirin, Layla and Majnun, The Seven Beauties,* and *Iskandar-nameh.*

Nizami never traveled beyond the region of Ganja, preferring his native land, which was the setting for several episodes in his narrative poems. Although he did not become a court poet, he was content to live on the small sums he received from the patrons he dedicated his poems to. Today he is recognized as an example of the amalgamation of Turkic and Iranian culture, and of Azerbaijan's contribution to it. *See also* LITERATURE, AZERI.

-O-

OGHUSIANISM. An offshoot of **Pan-Turkism** that emerged after the **Young Turkish Revolution** of 1908. In the view of its Turkish proponent, Ziya Gokalp, an alternative to the ideal of merging all Turks was the union of the peoples of the Oghuz subgroup of languages, uniting the **Azeris** and Turkmen, who were most closely related to the Ottoman Turks. Moreover, their unity, at least for the foreseeable future, would not be political, but rather purely cultural in nature. Thus, a new strain was added to Pan-Turkism, singling the Azeris out as the object of the Ottoman Turks' attention and serving as the basis for the special relationship of the two peoples. *See also* PAN-TURKISM.

OGHUZ TURKS. Federation of nomadic tribes of Central Asia from which the **Azeri** people trace their descent. In the eighth century the

Oghuz tribes made their way west to the steppes north of the **Caspian** and Aral Seas, in present-day Kazakhstan. Much of their early lifestyle is reflected in the epic cycle of stories The *Book of Dede Korkut,* which is considered a part of the Azeri literary heritage. The Oghuz were considered formidable fighters and were recruited into Islamic armies in large numbers as mercenaries. In the late 10th century the Oghuz converted to Islam and gave rise to the **Seljuk** dynasty. *See also* OGHU-SIANISM.

OIL INDUSTRY. Oil has been extracted on the western coast of Azerbaijan since before recorded history. A popular etymology of the name "Azerbaijan" traces it to the Persian word *azer* (fire), hence, Azerbaijan (land of fire) because of its ancient Zoroastrian temples with their fires fed by the plentiful local supplies of oil. In the extraction and processing of oil, the industrial age came only in the wake of the colonial conquest of the **Caspian** coast by Russia in the early 19th century. Even so, it took more than half a century before the elements of modern industrial production would emerge. Until the 1850s, the extraction of oil hovered at the stationary level of 250,000 *puds* (nine million pounds), a figure that, according to some estimates, was less than the output in the 10th century. The turning point came in 1872 with Russian legislation that changed the practice of granting oil concessions on crown lands into long-term leasing to the highest bidder.

This act of the colonial government, the most consequential one ever issued by the tsarist bureaucracy in Azerbaijan, threw opened the doors to mainly foreign investors with substantial capital to engage in large-scale mechanized production. Within a year of the reform, the first successful drilling replaced the old method of well-digging, and a gusher inaugurated the ascent of **Baku** to the rank of a major oil-producing center. Among the foreign investors, foremost was the Nobel Brothers Company, which would come to control more than half of the Baku oil output. Their chief competitors became the Paris Rothschilds, who in 1883 completed the construction of the railroad linking Baku with the Black Sea port of Batum. This feat provided Caspian oil access to world markets, and decreased the dependence on Russian markets.

The extraction of oil grew on an unparalleled scale, with Baku's output approaching that of the United States before the onset of the 1898 depression. But the ways in which the oil industry was allowed to operate soon began to claim prohibitive costs, the perennial feature for all of the periods of Russian rule. Chaotic or sloppy drilling and extraction led to a decline in the productive capacity. This condition was made worse by growing signs of political instability: early- 20th- century Baku became a major center of labor unrest in the Russian Empire, and the outbreak of the 1905 Revolution ushered in the wave of ethnic violence known as the **"Tatar-Armenian War."** By 1908 Baku no longer counted as a major factor in the world oil market.

Nonetheless, Baku retained its position as the supplier of the Russian market. Indeed, this position grew as the vagaries of history eliminated foreign competition. The onset of **World War I** brought a sharp increase in the prices of Caspian oil. In the closing months of the war, Baku and its oil fields were the prize coveted by all of the armies operating in Caucasia—Russian, Ottoman, German, and British. All of them saw control of Baku as the way to prolong or shorten the duration of the world conflict.

Oil wealth was regarded as the economic foundation of Azerbaijan's independence under the national government of the **Azerbaijani Democratic Republic** of 1918–1920, and the Baku regime made attempts at reorientation of oil exports from Russian to Western markets. These attempts were, however, frustrated by the steep decline in post-war prices. An additional reason for limited interest on the part of Western governments and companies in Caspian oil was their conviction that Russia, in whatever form it emerged from the Civil War, would reclaim its rule over the region. The oil-based economy that had grown as an appendage of Russia suffered a crisis when the Russian Civil War severed the links with Azerbaijan's traditional market, and oil exports fell precipitously to one-third of the preceding years' averages.

The Soviet period had all the markings of an intensified continuation of old trends in the Caspian oil industry, its output geared primarily to the Russian market. As time went on, exports that gained hard currency for Russia's industrialization effort were resumed. In the oil fields, there followed increasing overexploitation of resources, with investments invariably falling behind the rate of production. At the same time, the centrally planned pricing policy assured that any profits from oil production and export that remained in Azerbaijan were consistently modest.

World War II again brought to the fore the geopolitical dimension of the Baku oil fields' security. To stave off a threat from German agents in Iran, Soviet forces occupied the northern part of Iran. By far the greatest wartime threat to the flow of Baku oil to Russia came from the 1942 German offensive, which ultimately failed to penetrate the Caucasus barrier. During the war, Azerbaijan supplied 75 percent of the USSR's oil and 90 percent of its aviation fuel and lubrication oils.

As the Soviet epoch wore on, Baku's golden age of oil extraction receded into memory, partly as a result of the steady depletion of the onshore and shallow oil fields, but mostly because of underinvestment in exploration efforts. After World War II, as the west Caspian oil fields suffered from decline, new deposits were explored in the coastal Tengiz area of Kazakhstan, and then Turkmenistan. The center of gravity of Soviet oil extraction kept shifting, partly for strategic considerations, away from the Caspian borderland to the region between the Volga basin and the Ural Mountains, which became known as the "second Baku," and then, in the 1960s, to the west Siberian oil fields.

By the 1980s, Baku oil output would dwindle to a meager three percent of the Soviet total. Even though the republic still supplied most (70 percent) of the USRR's oil- and gas-producing equipment, some of the equipment used in the Baku oil fields dated back to the days of the Nobel Brothers Company. During the 1950–1978 period, Azerbaijan had the lowest rate of industrial growth among all of the Soviet republics.

With the oil industry's decline, Moscow's central planning authorities cut the flow of investment capital and technical assistance. The attempts to create replacements for the oil industry, such as the chemical complex in Sumgait or the promotion of large-scale **cotton cultivation,** produced limited economic effects but exacted high ecological costs.

Only in the twilight years of the Soviet Union did the condition of the oil industry become an openly voiced public concern in the emerging spirit of glasnost. The issue of the environmental crisis that was destroying the Caspian Sea was seen in conjunction with the depletion of natural resources, particularly oil—a condition that was keeping the peoples of the Caspian coast from joining the ranks of prosperous Middle Eastern nations. With Azerbaijani independence, the new regime of the **People's Front of Azerbaijan** made the oil industry a matter of its special concern, with wide-reaching implications. As in the years 1918–1920, it was believed that the oil industry could become a solid base on which to build the country's independence. While the onshore oil fields were depleted, Azerbaijan still had offshore deposits, though the costs of their exploitation would be higher. In Azerbaijan's sector of the Caspian Sea, huge reserves were identified, and estimates of potential resources were frequently revised upward. Taken as a whole, the oil deposits of the Caspian region came to be regarded as the second-richest in the world, after the Persian Gulf.

For all of the rosy prospects, the most pressing issue at the time was the lack of investment funds, the underlying cause of the oil industry's decline during the Soviet period. The condition had deteriorated so badly that the expenditures of extracting oil exceeded the income from it, and some two hundred wells remained out of commission for lack of repair funds. An influx of foreign investments, along with technology and management skills, appeared crucial for the very survival of Azerbaijan's oil industry; the new regime acted with dispatch to secure help from Western sources. Unlike 1919, there was no reluctance on the part of Western companies to negotiate a deal with an independent Azerbaijan.

In September 1992 two oil companies merged to form the Azerbaijani State Oil Company (SOCAR), and in the same month the agreement was concluded with a consortium that consisted of American, British, and Norwegian companies to develop the huge Azeri oil field. Preliminary agreements on other oil fields, Giunashli and Chiraq, were negotiated as well, and plans were made for laying a pipeline from the Caspian Sea to the Mediterranean coast of Turkey, the country with which the regime of Azerbaijans' president Abulfaz **Elchibey** was eager to establish a special relationship.

Understandably, the oil agreement, regarded as an opening to the West, caused dissatisfaction in Moscow. In early June, Azerbaijan experienced a classic Middle Eastern army coup launched by Colonel Surat **Huseynov,** who forced Elchibey to leave the capital. One of the first steps of the new president, Haidar **Aliyev** was to postpone the signing of the oil agreement, and to order its renegotiation. The highlight of the first year of his rule was the fashioning of a new oil deal. The difficult and protracted negotiations proceeded in the midst of the mounting "Caspian Sea controversy," a legal/political problem raised by a displeased Moscow.

The oil agreement, hailed as the "contract of the century," was signed on September 20, 1994, in Baku. The deal, covering 30 years and valued at more than seven billion dollars, was concluded with an enlarged consortium of foreign companies—four American (Amoco, Unocal, Pennzoil, and McDermott), one British (British Petroleum), one Norwegian (Statoil), one Turkish (TPAO), and the Russian company, Lukoil. Iran was absent from the consortium, and when Teheran later attempted to join, its bid was rejected at the insistence of American companies, which in this case seemed to have followed the wishes of the U.S. State Department.

The inclusion of a Russian company in the consortium was understood as a means of allaying Moscow's fears of a large Western presence in the Caspian area. Moscow barely concealed its displeasure, and in an official statement declared that unilateral actions by any state regarding the Caspian Sea were illegal and would be opposed. Within less than two weeks there followed another attempt at a coup, this time unsuccessful, against Aliyev. The oil agreement survived along with his regime, but the issue of routing the pipelines and natural gas was becoming a major controversy and the new focal point of Caspian oil politics: Should the pipelines pass through the territory of Russia, the power that had lost direct control over the Caspian oil fields but still has a vested interest in controling the flow of fuel exports to the West? Or should the pipelines bypass Russian territory entirely, thereby reducing Moscow's ability to control the flow?

Eight other oil agreements followed the contract of the century, allowing for the exploitation and development of the Karabagh and Shah Deniz fields. Meanwhile, current oil production had to be transported through the existing facilities. Of the available options—the western route via Georgia to the Black Sea, or the northern route via Russian territory to Novorossiysk—the latter gained preference. On November 12, 1997, President Aliyev opened a valve on a platform in the sea, making the first "early oil" flow through the pipeline to Novorossiysk. At the present time, Baku has concluded deals worth more than 40 billion dollars, and Azerbaijan's offshore fields are expected to produce oil worth 100 billion dollars over the next 30 years. Even though the route through which to transport the "big oil" has not been decided on, the expectations for the year 2000 are that oil exports will be at high levels. Initially, Azerbaijan will keep only about a third of the profits, and the rest will be used for recovery of capital by foreign investors. After the year 2005, these investors will have recovered their capital and Azerbaijan's share of profits will rise to five-sixths.

Meanwhile, the figures for the proven reserves have been lowered from the initial estimate of close to 200 billion barrels. Some test drillings were disappointing, and the worldwide decline in oil prices put on hold the construction of the main export pipeline to the Mediterranean coast. The euphoric spirit of the Second Baku Boom has been dampened as some companies have begun to rethink their Caspian ventures. Most investors, however, are willing to stay, in expectation of the price recovery from its unusually low level of $10 a barrel. *See also* ECONOMY; PIPELINE POLITICS; REPUBLIC OF AZERBAIJAN.

OZAKOM (OSOBYI ZAKAVKAZSKII KOMITET). The Special Transcaucasian Committee that was created by the prime minister of Russia, Prince Lvov, on March 9, 1917, following the overthrow of tsar Nicholas II. The committee was to act as the Petrograd provisional government's agent in **Transcaucasia,** and was meant to represent the national groups of the region. Its chairman was a Russian Consitutional Democrat, V. A. Kharlamov, and its other deputies were A. I. Chkhenkeli, a Georgian Menshevik; Prince K. Abashidze, a Georgian Social Federalist; M. I. Papadjanian, an Armenian Kadet; and M. Y. Jafarov, an Azeri with no party affiliation, subsequently a Musavatist. The Ozakom never wielded much power in Transcaucasia, but it functioned as a court of appeals when disagreements between governmental bodies could not be locally resolved. The Ozakom was dissolved following the Bolshevik coup against the provisional government in October 1917 and was replaced with the **Transcaucasian Commissariat.** *See also* TRANSCAUCASIAN COMMISSARIAT.

-P-

PAN-ISLAMISM. A movement calling for the unity of Muslim peoples regardless of their ethnic, national, or sectarian distinctions. It dominated the political thinking of the Azeri **intelligentsia** in the late 19th and early 20th century. Pan-Islamism emerged as an Islamic response to the encroachments of Europe, and addressed itself to the collective consciousness of the *'umma,* the worldwide community of believers in Islam.

Primarily a defensive reaction to the pressures of the outside world, Pan-Islamism failed to develop into a uniform doctrine. There was more than one version of Pan-Islamism. The call for the world's Muslims to close ranks around the Ottoman sultan, who also used the title of "caliph," was in fact a foreign policy instrument of the Abdulhamid II regime.

Hajji Sayyid al-Afghani (d. 1897), an Iranian-born writer and scholar, preached a liberal variety of Pan-Islamism. He believed in Islam's compatibility with reason, and urged Muslims to adopt, albeit selectively, Western techniques and methods. Al-Afghani exhorted his coreligionists to rid themselves of dogmatism, fatalism, superstitions, and passivity and to overcome sectarian strife. At the same time, he advised Muslims to use nationalism as a weapon against colonialism, and he believed in eventual unification of all Islamic peoples under one rule, which would be constitutional and liberal rather than despotic, as was the Ottoman state. Young **Azeris** found al-Afghani's brand of Pan-Islamism appealing and were especially drawn by the prospect of a Shi'a-Sunni reconciliation in an ecumenical spirit of modernized Islam. Moreover, it made it easier for them to cultivate the historical bond to Iran. *See also* INTELLIGENTSIA.

PAN-TURKISM. The movement for cultural unity and cooperation of Turkic peoples of the world. In its initial stage Pan-Turkism spread mainly among the intellectuals of the Turkic population in the Russian empire. Its leading proponent was a Crimean Tatar, Ismail bey **Gaspirali (Gasprinski)** who published the newspaper *Tarjuman* (Interpreter). His motto was "unity of thought, language, and action," and on the pages of his newspaper he tried to forge a standard literary idiom for all of the Turkic peoples based on simplified Ottoman. Other pioneers of Pan-Turkism in the Russian-held lands were the Tatar Yusuf Akchuraoghlu and the Azeri Ali bey **Huseynzade.** In the Ottoman state, Pan-Turkism began to spread rapidly after the 1908 **Young Turkish Revolution** where it also acquired a political coloring. Among the Ottomans, the chief proponent of Pan-Turkism became Ziya Gokalp.

An offshoot of Pan-Turkism was Turanism, the program of political unification of Turkic peoples under the Ottoman aegis, one of the aims of Turkey in **World War I.** In the closing months of the war, the Ottoman forces succeeded in seizing both Russian and **Iranian Azerbaijan,** but the prospect of being joined to the Ottoman Empire caused frictions with the local political elites. With the coming to power of Mustafa Kemal in Turkey, Pan-Turkism was officially repudiated in Turkey, though it has continued as a trend in Turkish political thinking. In Azerbaijan, where Pan-Turkism was generally accepted among the political and intellectual elite, the experience of the 1918 Ottoman occupation started the process of redefining Pan-Turkism as a cultural rather than political program. *See also* GASPIRALI, ISMAIL, BEY; HUSEYNZADE, ALI, BEY; OGHUSIANISM.

PARAMILITARY POLICE UPRISING. An armed uprising against the government of the **Republic of Azerbaijan** broke out on March 13, 1995. Led by Deputy Interior Minister Rovshan Javadov, a 3,000-man paramilitary police unit began a rebellion a few miles north of **Baku,** calling for the removal of President Haidar **Aliyev.** The rebels were foiled by government forces loyal to Aliyev who repulsed an attempted capture of the presidential palace by 700 insurgents on March 17. During the suppression of the rebellion, Deputy Interior Minister Javadov was killed, along with a number of the rebels. Aliyev blamed the uprising on ex-President Ayaz **Mutalibov** and ex-Prime Minister Surat **Huseynov,** who were helping those in Moscow who wished to destabilize Azerbaijan in order to gain control over its oil wealth. Another foreign link that subsequently came into public view was the one with the organized crime in Turkey. *See also* ALIYEV HAIDAR; REPUBLIC OF AZERBAIJAN.

PEOPLE'S FRONT OF AZERBAIJAN (PFAz). The main opposition force to the Soviet regime in the period of its final decline. The PFAz was born at the initiative of a handful of intellectuals including Araz Alizade, Layla Iunusova, Hikmat Hajizade, Tofiq Gasymov, Isa Gambar, and Aydin Balayev, who set up an association in support of perestroika. The constituent conference of the Front met in June 1989, but prior to the leaders' deliberations, grassroot sentiments had resulted in some 200 PFAz cells in **Baku**, and 70 percent of all students considered themselves to be PFAz sympathizers.

The Front's program amounted to the most comprehensive statement of Azeri aspirations to emerge from Russian totalitarian rule. It focused on what appeared to be the issues of fundamental significance for the community, ranging from economic reforms to the environment, religious freedom, and symbols of national identity.

The strain of eclectism in the PFAz's declarations reflected its open-door attitude of accepting the followers of all political trends, including the Communists. Despite, or on account of, this all-inclusive quality, the PFAz rapidly became Azerbaijan's major center of political influence, and the head of the **Communist Party of Azerbaijan,** Abdul Rakhman **Vazirov,** felt compelled in the fall of 1989 to conclude a series of agreements with the PFAz leadership.

Although the PFAz could at that time regard itself as one of the most powerful movements of its kind in any of the Soviet republics, diverse political orientations undermined its cohesion. By the end of 1989, the Front effectively became split into three wings known as liberal, national-liberationist, and Islamic. Some leaders could not find a place for themselves in any of these wings and left the ranks of the Front. Early in January 1990, the leadership of the PFAz passed temporarily into the hands of the group that included Etibar Mammadov, Rahim Gaziyev, and Abulfaz Aliyev, and rejected the principle of moderation as the political guideline. The PFAz's position in the Baku 1990 **Black January** Days provided the measure of its disunity. Many reports agreed that the PFAz activists sometimes risked their own lives to protect the **Armenians,** but there were also reports that other members of the Front remained passive, inciting, or even committing, acts of violence.

After the January Days, the pace of the PFAz's decline seemed to quicken, especially given that hundreds of its activists were under arrest, including Etibar Mammadov, the head of the executive committee. In the September 30, 1990, parliamentary elections, held amidst widely reported violations, the PFAz ran as a part of the Democratic Bloc, an alliance that received only 26 out of 350 mandates. No candidate from the Front's leadership was elected to the Supreme Soviet.

Yet, as the decline of the USSR was progressing, the opposition appeared to be losing battles even while it was winning the war. The Front showed revived strength in the street protests against President Ayaz **Mutalibov's** backing for the August 19, 1991, coup in Moscow, and was again recognized as a major political force in the newly created **National Council,** the legislative body with half of its membership consisting of the opposition.

The PFAz was instrumental in bringing down the presidency of Mutalibov in March 1992, and even more in defeating his attempt to recover power in May. In the upsurge of the Front's fortunes, its leader, Abulfaz **Elchibey,** became the first democratically elected president of Azerbaijan in June 1992.

The PFAz's ascendancy ended within a year under the combined impact of military defeats in the **Nagorno-Karabagh dispute,** a deepening economic crisis, and worsening relations with Russia. The Elchibey presidency was overthrown by the military coup of Colonel Surat **Huseynov.** Under the regime of Haidar **Aliyev,** the PFAz returned to the role of an opposition group, changing its name to the Party of the People's Front of Azerbaijan (PPFAz). *See also* ELCHIBEY, ABULFAZ; NAGORNO-KARABAGH DISPUTE; REPUBLIC OF AZERBAIJAN.

PIPELINE POLITICS. With the concluding of the mid-1990s oil agreements, which opened the way for foreign investment funds, the focus shifted to the problem of safely and economically exporting the oil to world markets. Pipeline politics boiled down to the choice of the most suitable route, or routes, given the region's geopolitical situation and its chronic lack of security. As to the geopolitics of **Caucasia,** there could be no doubt that Russia would remain a primary factor in any equation.

The position of Moscow toward the **Caspian Sea** oil could be summarized as follows: the Western investments would revive production, with Russia deriving income from the pipeline fees and and retaining strategic control over the flow of oil. Such an arrangement was not acceptable to the Western companies and their respective governments. Still, it was in everyone's best interest to offer Russia a stake in successful cooperation. From this assumption, there emerged the compromise plan of not one, but two pipeline systems—one carrying the "early oil" from the current production in a limited volume and including the route linking **Baku** with the Russian Black Sea port Novorossiysk, either passing through the territory of Chechnya or, should it again be affected by political instability, bypassing it. Another "early oil" route, a 515-mile-long pipeline to the Georgian port of Supsa, was opened in April 1999. This shorter and less costly pipeline remains outside of direct Russian control, although it could be threatened by Abkhazian secessionist movements.

The "big oil" route is as yet undecided; in fact the final decision is being postponed in view of the sharp fall of oil prices. The U.S. government position is that reliance on too few pipelines should be avoided, and that the preferred outlet should be Ceyhan on the Mediterranean coast of Turkey. But the high construction costs would be reflected in the prices, making the Caspian oil less competitive in the world market.

Another alternative, the southern route through Iran to the Persian Gulf, remains even less likely, given the state of relations between Teheran and Washington. On U.S. insistence, Iran was excluded from participation in the consortium as well as from the pipeline negotiations. In the "sea or lake" Caspian controversy, Teheran took the side of Russia, yet it does not share its position on the pipeline routes. Iran's interest lies in attracting the lucrative oil transport from the Caspian and Central Asia to its territory, a prospect that would weaken the powerful Russian influence in these regions. Although this alternative is not realistic at the present time, at some point, when Iran–U.S. relations have improved, the participation of Iran in the pipeline system may prove to be a crucial element of stability and security for **Transcaucasia,** and particularly Azerbaijan. *See also* ECONOMY; OIL INDUSTRY.

PISHEVARI, JAFAR SAYYID (JAVADZADE KHALKALI, 1892–1947). A prominent figure in the Iranian Communist movement. Born in Khalkal, **Iranian Azerbaijan,** he moved to **Baku** in his youth, where he was exposed to revolutionary influences. He was one of the founders of the **Adalat** Party in 1916. A prolific journalist, he contributed to Baku leftist newspapers. In 1920 he joined the government of the Communist-led Gilan Republic as the interior commissar. He spent the years 1931 to 1941 in Iranian prisons for his Communist activities. After his release, Pishevari founded the leftist newspaper, *Azhir,* in which he criticized the Iranian Tudeh Party as being too sectarian. Elected in 1944 to Iran's 14th Majlis, he was prevented from serving in the parliament when his credentials were rejected. In the fall of 1945, he was one of the founding members of the **Democratic Party of Azerbaijan** (DPAz), which absorbed the local chapters of the Tudeh and the labor unions. With Soviet help the DPAz formed the **Autonomous Government of Azerbaijan,** with Pishevari at its head. After the USSR abandoned the DPAz and the Iranian army put an end to the autonomous government in November 1946, Pishevari and other leaders of the party went into exile in Baku. Here his disagreements with the head of the **Communist Party of Azerbaijan,** Mir Jafar **Baghirov,** became public knowledge, as Pishevari emphasized his attachment to Iran. In July 1947, he died as the result of an automobile accident, its circumstances implicating Baghirov. *See also* ADALAT; AUTONOMOUS GOVERNMENT OF AZERBAIJAN; DEMOCRATIC PARTY OF AZERBAIJAN (1945–1960).

PRESS. Native language newspaper publishing in Azerbaijan dates back to Hasan bey **Zardabi's Akinchi (Ploughman)** in 1875. After this newspaper was closed down by the tsarist authorities during the Russo-Ottoman War of 1877, the **Azeri** press found continuity in the small-circulation magazines *Ziya* (Dawn, 1879–1881) and *Ziya-i Kafkasiyya* (The Caucasian Dawn, 1881–1884), and the literary review *Kashkul* (The Darwish Bowl, 1884–1891). After the publication of *Kashkul* was banned by the government, the Azeri **language** press was not revived until the eve of the Russian Revolution of 1905 with the newspaper *Sharq-i Rus* (The Russian East), founded in 1903 by Mammad Agha Shahtakhtinski.

In the new period of relaxed government controls **Baku** became the leading center of Muslim journalism throughout the Russian Empire. In the years 1905–1917, no less than 63 newspapers and periodicals were in circulation at one time or another. Some of these represented high journalistic or intellectual standards, such as the dailies *Hayat* (*Life*), *Irshad* (Guidance), the literary review *Fuyuzat* (Abundance), and the most widely circulated of all—the satirical-literary magazine, *Molla Nasr al-din.*

The Soviet period brought the demise of the independent press, but with the expansion of the reading public, specialized periodicals in various fields made their appearance under a growing number of titles. The main daily newspaper of the Soviet Azerbaijani Republic was the Russian language *Bakinskii Rabochii* (Baku Worker), the press organ of the **Communist Party of Azerbaijan.**

The pent-up intellectual, artistic, and political energies of the Azeris were released with the coming of glasnost, and newspaper publishing experienced a new efflorescence. The newspapers—legal, semilegal, and underground—published in the late 1980s multiplied, even though many turned out to be short-lived. Among the best known were *Azadlyq* (Freedom), the publication of the **People's Front of Azerbaijan;** *Istiqlal* (Independence), the newspaper of the Social-Democrats; *Azarbayjan, Novruz* (New Day); *Otlar Yurdu* (The Land of Fires); and *Elm* (Knowledge). Under the **Aliyev** regime, censorship was partly restored in 1993 on the grounds of the **Nagorno-Karabagh** war, and some journalists were arrested. The censorship was relaxed before the 1995 parliamentary elections.

The independent press of Azerbaijan has remained an important forum for Azeri civil society. *Azadlyq* is still one of the largest-circulation newspapers. Among publications appearing weekly or twice a week, the leading titles include *Ayna-Zerkalo* (Mirror), *7 Giun* (Seven Days), *Hurriyet* (Freedom), and the Russian language *Panoroma.*

In the post 1993 period, a countrywide press debate was launched on the concept of the Azerbaijani "national idea." The discussion included topics of special relevance to the public conciousness: maintaining independence; freedom versus order; democracy versus Big Brother; human rights versus national values; the extent of free trade; the timeliness and relevance of the slogan "Turkism, Modernization, and Islam;" modernization with, or without, Westernization. *See also* INTELLIGENTSIA; LITERATURE.

-Q-

QAJARS. The name of the royal dynasty ruling over Iran from 1794 to 1925. Its founder was Agha Muhammad, a leader of the Turkmen Qajar tribe, who reunified Iran after the period of fragmentation under the Zand dynasty, and tried to assert Iranian sovereignity over **Caucasia,** including Georgia and Azerbaijan. He was crowned shah in 1796, to be succeeded the next year by his nephew, Fath Ali Shah (1797–1834). Fath Ali Shah tried to challenge the Russian conquest of the lands south of the **Caucasus** range, but met with defeats in two wars (1804–1813 and 1826–1828) losing Caucasia north of the **Araxes–Kura** line.

The 1828 **Turkmanchai Treaty** provided Russia with growing economic and political influence in Iran, a process counteracted by Britain. The rivalry between the two European powers was exploited to Iran's benefit by the most successful of the Qajar rulers, Nasr ul-din (1848–1896). Under his long reign, Iran saw the beginnings of modernization. Its progress, however, was slow and inconsistent. His successor, Muzaffar ul-din (1896–1907) was forced to grant the constitution that introduced the *Majlis* (parliament) and limited the royal power. An attempt to rescind the constitution by his successor, Muhammad Ali (1907–1909) led to the outbreak of civil war and his deposition. The Qajar period reached its deepest decline with the last monarch of the dynasty, Ahmad Shah (1909–1925), under whose reign Iran experienced occupation by Russian and British and, during **World War I,** Ottoman troops.

The weakness and disintegration that continued in Iran after the war were the backdrop for the emergence of a strong leader who held the promise of pulling the country from its sorry condition. Colonel Reza Khan in 1921 forced Ahmad Shah to appoint him to the command of the army. In 1925 he induced the Majlis to depose the Qajar royal family and to crown him as the founder of the new, Pahlavi dynasty. *See also* IRANIAN AZERBAIJAN; IRANIAN CONSTITUTIONAL REVOLUTION.

QARA-QOYUNLU (BLACK SHEEP). A federation of nomadic Turco-Mongolian tribes. Their name was derived from the black sheep on their banner. The Qara-Qoyunlu were led by the Baharlu tribe and were originally settled in the Lake Van region. The tribe supported the Ottoman Turks and the Jelairids, and fought against the forces of Tamerlane and his allies, the **Aq-Qoyunlu.** After Tamerlane's death in 1405, the tribe assisted the Jelairids in the defeat of his son Miranshah. They later turned on the Jalairids and defeated them, taking possession of Azerbaijan, Iraq, and Armenia in 1410. The Qara-Qoyunlu fought against the Timurids and the **Shirvanshahs,** but were defeated in 1435 and forced to become vassals of the Timurids. Between 1453 and 1457, the Qara-Qoyunlu conquered western Iran, and in 1457, after the death of the Timurid ruler Shahrukh, they declared their independence. In 1468 the Qara-Qoyunlu were decisively defeated by the armies of the Aq-Qoyunlu and absorbed by their state. *See also* AQ-QOYUNLU.

QIZILBASH (REDHEADS) The members of the Turkmen tribes who wore red headgear to demonstrate their support for the founders of the **Safavid** kingdom. They were the chief armed force of the early Safavid Shi'ite rule and participated in attacks on neighboring non-Muslim countries, including Georgia and the Trebizond Empire. The Qizilbashi destroyed the **Aq-Qoyunlu** state at the beginning of the 16th century. Their military leader, Ismail Safavid (**Ismail I,** 1486–1524), was proclaimed shah and founded the Safavid kingdom in 1501. Initially, the chief officials of the Safavids came from the ranks of the Qizilbash aristocracy. Their importance declined sharply after the creation of a regular army under the reforms of Shah **Abbas** I in the late 16th century. *See also* ABBAS I, SHAH (1588–1629).

QULUZADE MAMMAD JALIL (1866–1932). A prominent Azeri writer and journalist. A graduate of the teachers training college in Gori, he took to journalism in the newspaper *Sharq-i rus* published in Tbilisi, in 1903–1904. In 1906, in the midst of the Russian Revolution, he founded the satirical-literary journal *Molla Nasr al-din,* which enjoyed the largest circulation of all Azeri language press publications, and served as the model for satirical journals in Iran and Turkey. In the pages of *Molla Nasr al-din,* Mammmad Quluzade commented on the issues of the day and the revolutionary developments in Russia, Iran, and Turkey, and campaigned vigorously against attempts at Ottomanization of the literary **language** of Azerbaijan. Following the Soviet seizure of **Baku** in 1920, he left for **Tabriz** where he briefly restored the publication of *Molla Nasr al-din* after a hiatus of several years. Invited by the Soviet regime, he returned to Baku in 1922. Apart from journalistic articles and feuilletons, he wrote plays, novels, short stories, and essays. *See also* AZARIJILAR; LITERATURE; *MOLLA NASR AL-DIN.*

-R-

RASULZADE, MAMMAD AMIN (1884–1954). A statesman, writer, and journalist, who is generally recognized as the most outstanding figure of 20th-century non-Communist **Azeri** political life. He was one of the founders of the **Himmat Party,** and his activities in the 1905–1907 Revolution brought him into contact with Joseph Stalin. After the Revolution had run its course, Rasulzade, along with other Himmatists, emigrated to Iran to take part in the constitutional revolution currently under way in that country. He became one of the prominent members of the radical-reformist Democrat Party and editor in chief of the first European style Iranian daily newspaper, *Iran-i nou.*

In 1912, following the Russian military intervention in Iran, he was forced to leave for Istanbul, now the center of the **Pan-Turkish** movement under the **Young Turks'** regime. His stay in Istanbul ended with the tsarist amnesty of 1913, which allowed him to return home. In **Baku,** Rasulzade joined the clandestine **Musavat Party**, but concentrated on open journalism. In 1915, he received permission to publish the native language newspaper *Achiq soz* (*The Open Word*), which called itself Turkic while endorsing the official Russian war on patriotism against Ottoman Turkey. Following the overthrow of Tsar Nicholas II, Rasulzade emerged in the spring of 1917 as the undisputed leader of the Musavat Party, and in his speeches in the forum of the all-Russian Muslim movement acted as the spokesman for the assertion of national identities of Turkic peoples—a position contrary to the views of the **Pan-Islamists,** and even some Pan-Turkists. On the platform of nascent Azeri nationalism, the Musavat merged in the fall of 1917 with the **Ganja**-based **Turkic Party of Decentralization,** and Rasulzade became the head of the unified party's Central Committee.

Upon the formation of the **Azerbaijani National Council** on May 28, 1918, he was elected its chairman. In this capacity he came to contend with the Ottoman military authorities, which tended to regard

Azerbaijan as a prospective part of Turkey. Under Ottoman pressure, the National Council dissolved itself, and Rasulzade left Azerbaijan for an invitational visit to Istanbul from which he returned at the end of the war. In the post-war period of the **Azerbaijani Democratic Republic** he held no governmental position, though he wielded influence as the leader of the Musavat, in which he was identified with its Left, or Baku, wing. Unlike the Ganja or Right wing, the Left was perceived as more accommodating to the Bolsheviks, and after the Red Army's invasion of Azerbaijan, Rasulzade was personally freed from imprisonment by his old acquaintance, Stalin. Yet Stalin decided to give him employment in the Commissariat of Nationalitics Affairs in Moscow rather than allowing him to remain in Azerbaijan.

In 1922, Rasulzade managed to leave Russia to resume the life of a political refugee. His first country of exile was Turkey, where he combined activities in émigré politics with work as a writer and journalist. His unwillingness to accept restrictions or guidance from the Kemalist regime gained him expulsion from Turkey, and in 1930 he moved to Poland, a country whose government had for some years been supporting the activities of the émigrés from the USSR through the Promethean movement. The 1936 congress of the Musavat held in Warsaw confirmed the position of Rasulzade as the party leader.

The outbreak of the German-Soviet war in 1941 found Rasulzade in Rumania. Here, was invited to Berlin for talks on Azeri political representation on the German side. In his negotiations with the Germans, he insisted that the Reich should first declare its unconditional commitment to the restoration of the independence of the **Transcaucasian** states. When his hosts acted evasively, he left Berlin.

After the end of the war, Rasulzade lived for some time in the Western-occupied parts of Germany, from where he made his way to post-Kemalist Turkey, which granted him refuge for the rest of his life. He died there in 1954. *See also* MUSAVAT.

RAWWADID DYNASTY. A dynasty of Arab origin from the Yemeni tribe of Azd. In the early Abbasid period the Rawwadids were governors of **Tabriz.** Abu l-Hayja Rawwadid drove the Rawwadid **Musafarid** dynasty from most of their **Transcaucasian** lands by 984. Although the Rawwadid dynasty successfully coped with the first incursions of the **Oghuz Turks,** in 1054 they submitted to the armies of Tughril and became vassals of the **Seljuks.** In 1071 Alp Arslan put an end to the dynasty by deposing the Rawwadid ruler Mamlan Wahsudan. *See also* MUSAFARID DYNASTY.

REPUBLIC OF AZERBAIJAN. The present-day Republic of Azerbaijan was formed following the break-up of the Soviet Union in August 1991. The Communist-dominated Azerbaijani Supreme Soviet voted unanimously to restore Azerbaijan's independent status on August 30. The declaration of independence signaled Azerbaijan's eagerness for international recognition, but at the same time it indicated its closeness to the heritage of the USSR. The meaning of independence was still not clear, as the declaration did not spell out the secession, and high officials continued to castigate unnamed separatists.

According to tradition dating to the late Soviet period, the politically articulate class in Azerbaijan consisted of two main segments: one was the nomenklatura, the Communist Party members selected to form a pool of candidates for high executive positions in the government, administration, and economic management. The other segment was the **intelligentsia.** The two groups, one monopolizing power, the other excluded from it, were in a state of anatagonism that became public in the post-Soviet period. Moreover, the new historical circumstances brought to light fissures within each group. The overall effect was political instability, and within the first seven years of its existence, the republic of Azerbaijan has had three presidents, two acting presidents, and two successful and at least as many unsuccessful coup d'etats. At the same time the composition of the elite has been undergoing changes with the rise of political parties, a process that generated an influx of professional politicians, as well as the entry into political life of members of emerging middle classes and business interests.

Post-Soviet independence divides into three distinct phases, each marked by a different presidency, whose holder was, as in most of the post-Soviet republics, given extensive powers. Ayaz **Mutalibov's** reelection in September 1991 in the purely Soviet style with 98.5 percent majority was seen as a barely disguised continuation of the nomenklatura's rule. By contrast, his successor, Abulfaz **Elchibey,** symbolized the victory of the intelligentsia-led democratic and national forces opposed to communism. In turn, the coming to power of Haidar **Aliyev** heralded the return to relative stability under the rule of a reformed, enlarged, and rejuvenated nomenklatura.

Among the multitude of problems that the Republic of Azerbaijan has had to contend with in its emergence from the Soviet past, two stood out as the leading themes of the independence period, with their complex ramifications. The **Nagorno-Karabagh dispute** resulted in military defeat for Azerbaijan, with the loss of a fifth of its territory and a mass of war refugees. The defeat also put an end to the presidencies of Mutalibov and Elchibey. The Karabagh war was stopped by the 1994 cease-fire agreement, under the presidency of Aliyev, without, however, bringing a political solution.

The other leading theme of post-Soviet independence has been the revival of the **oil industry,** a process that gained momentum with the agreement signed in 1994 with a group of international companies for exploration of Azerbaijani oil deposits. Hailed as the Contract of the Century, the agreement resulted in a flow of Western investments, which in turn helped the republic under the Elchibey and Aliyev presidencies to follow a generally Western-oriented foreign policy—all the more so given that Moscow continued militarily assisting Armenia. The oil industry's revival, clearly a promising sign for the country's future has not meant prosperity for the population at large, which still suffers from a low standard of living. Meanwhile, the regime's electoral practices produce growing restivness among the opposition groups and postpone Azerbaijan's acceptance into the European Union. *See also* NAGORNO-KARABAGH DISPUTE; OIL INDUSTRY; PEOPLE'S FRONT OF AZERBAIJAN.

RUSSO-IRANIAN WAR, FIRST (1804–1813). Following the consolidation of power in Iran by the **Qajar** dynasty, Iran attempted to regain control of northern Azerbaijan. In 1804, Fath Ali Shah of Iran sent an army under the command of his son, Abbas Mirza, to invade Russian-held Azerbaijan. The force quickly met with defeat at the battle of Etchmiadzin and withdrew. In 1806 a second invasion, aided by revolts in **Sheki** and **Karabagh,** was also repulsed by the Russians, who proceeded to subdue the khanates of **Baku** and **Kuba.** The **Talysh** Khanate fell to Russian forces in 1809. Following the conclusion of a concurrent war with Ottoman Turkey in 1812, the Russians brought their full forces to bear on Iran. After a brief and successful Russian campaign, the 1813 Treaty of **Gulistan** was signed in which Iran acknowledged the Russian occupation of northern Azerbaijan and renounced its sovereignty over the khanates of Karabagh, Baku, Sheki, **Shirvan,** Kuba, and **Derbent.** *See also* GULISTAN, TREATY OF (1813); RUSSO-IRANIAN WAR, SECOND (1826–1828).

RUSSO-IRANIAN WAR, SECOND (1826–1828). The Second Russo-Iranian War broke out in May 1826 when Fath Ali Shah again sent his army, under the command of Prince Abbas Mirza, to invade the region of the **Caucasus.** The Iranian army occupied Lenkoran, Shemakha, and Nukha while besieging the Russian garrison at Shusha. The khan of **Talysh** started a rebellion in support of the Iranians. Despite being fellow Muslims, some **Azeris** fought for the Russian forces against the **Qajar** army. The battle of **Ganja** was a decisive defeat for the Iranian forces and marked the turning point of the war. Russian forces were able to clear the Caucasus of the shah's troops and push on as far as **Tabriz,** which they occupied. With the road to Teheran open, Fath Ali Shah sued for peace, and on February 10, 1828, the Treaty of **Turkmanchai** ended the war. The treaty, whose architect was the Russian oriental scholar Alexandr **Griboedov,** restated the earlier Treaty of **Gulistan** provisions, but, in addition, the shah was forced to cede the rights to the khanates of **Erivan** and **Nakhichevan.** Russia also secured capitulatory privileges in Iran, a country that would from then on become the target of Russian economic penetration. The Turkmanchai Treaty passed into history as the event marking the permanent division of Azerbaijan and its people, who thenceforth would live in two vastly different empires. *See also* GULISTAN, TREATY OF (1813); RUSSO-IRANIAN WAR, FIRST (1804–1813); TURKMANCHAI, TREATY OF (1828).

RUSSO-OTTOMAN WAR (1828–1829). Armed conflict between Russia and the Ottoman state broke out a few months after the conclusion of the Treaty of **Turkmanchai,** which ended the Second **Russo-Iranian War.** One of Russia's aims was to secure its hold over the newly gained possessions in **Caucasia.** Russian forces advanced into Ottoman territory taking Ardahan, Bayezit, Kars, and Erzerum. Another army operating in Europe seized Varna and Burgas on the Black Sea, crossed the Balkan Mountains, and entered Adrianople (Edirne). Defeated on all fronts, the Ottomans sued for peace. The resulting Treaty of Adrianople (1829) returned Erzerum, Kars, and Bayezit to the Ottoman state, but awarded parts of Georgia to Russia. By winning the eastern coast of the Black Sea, Russia firmly established its strategic control over Caucasia.

-S-

SABIR, ALEKPAR (1862–1911). Pen name of Mirza Alekpar Tairzade, a leading **Azeri** poet of the early 20th century who became known as the bard of the age of revolution. Initially an author of lyrical *ghazellas,* Sabir turned to politically motivated themes with the outbreak of the Russian Revolution of 1905. He found further sources of inspiration in the **Iranian Constitutional Revolution** of 1906–1911, and the **Young Turkish Revolution** of 1908. Both of these events were amply reflected in his poetry. His poems were circulated by the literary-satirical journal *Molla Nasr al-din,* enjoying wide popularity in both Russian and **Iranian Azerbaijan.** *See also* LITERATURE; *MOLLA NASR AL-DIN.*

SAFAVID DYNASTY. An originally **Azeri** dynasty founded by Shah **Ismail I** of Iran (1501–1524) following his victory over the **Aq-Qoyunlu.** The Safavid state existed from 1502 until 1736 and comprised Iran, Azerbaijan, parts of Armenia, most of Afghanistan, and Iraq. The power base of the first Safavid shahs was the **Qizilbash** tribes from which its army was recruited. Its capital was **Tabriz** until 1555, when it was moved to Qavzin. It was moved again in 1597 to Isfahan.

Long wars fought against the Ottoman Turks and the Uzbek khans, and heavy taxation resulted in rebellions in Gīlān in 1570–1571 and in Tabriz in 1571–1573. This domestic disorder led to the fragmentation of the Safavid state, and loss of the northwestern regions to the Ottomans, and Khorāsān to the Uzbeks. Facing the total disintegration of their state, the Qizilbash nobility, along with Kurdish and Lur elite as well as the Shi'ite clergy, joined in support of Shah **Abbas I** (1588–1629).

Winning a series of victories over the invaders, Abbas I recovered Azerbaijan, Khorasan, and Iraq. The kingdom was further strengthened by reforms of the taxation system, the state administration, and the military. Revenues from captured domains were used to maintain a standing army. With these improvements the Safavid state grew in strength and enjoyed an economic upsurge.

Economic and political decline set in during the 18th century due to government mismanagement and rising taxes. Rebellions flared within the state, and lands were lost to foreign conquest. Isfahan was captured by Afghan tribes in 1722, **Caucasia** and western Iran were lost to the Ottomans, and the **Caspian** regions were ceded to Russia by Shah Tahmasp II (1722–1732). The Safavid dynasty was overthrown by the military commander **Nadir Shah Afshar** in 1736. *See also* AQ-QOYUNLU; QIZILBASH.

SAFAVIDS (SAFAWIYYAH). A Sufi dervish order founded in the late 13th century by Shaikh Safi al-Din (1252–1334) in the city of Ardabil in **Iranian Azerbaijan.** The order created an army made up largely of the **Qizilbash,** who were used to defeat the **Aq-Qoyunlu** in 1499. This victory eventually led to the rise of the Safavid state. *See also* AQ-QOYUNLU; QIZILBASH.

SATTAR KHAN (1867–1914). A horse dealer by profession who became a revolutionary leader of **Iranian Azerbaijan**—often compared with his contemporary, Emiliano Zapata of Mexico. Having gained experience in guerrilla warfare against the royal forces, he took the command of the 1908 **Tabriz** uprising against the attempt to restore absolutism by Shah Muhammad Ali. A gifted military leader with charismatic qualities, Sattar Khan became a legendary hero of Azerbaijan on both sides of the frontier. *See also* IRANIAN CONSTITUTIONAL REVOLUTION; TABRIZ.

SELJUKS. The name of a family of **Oghuz Turks,** who established several dynasties throughout the Middle East. The founder of the first of the Seljuk dynasties was Tughril, who seized Khorāsān in 1037 and Baghdad in 1055. His successor, Alp Arslan, founded the sultanate of Rum and brought under his control Armenia and all of Iran, including Azerbaijan. The process of ethnic and linguistic Turkification of Azerbaijan began during the Seljuk period. As a frontier province, Azerbaijan developed traditions of *ghazi* warfare (fighting for the Faith). The Seljuk hold over Iran, undermined by internal feuds, was dealt the final blow by the state of the Khwarezm Shahs, an aggressive power that arose in northeast Iran in the 12th century.

SEPTEMBER MASSACRE OF 1918. Outbreak of violence against the **Armenian** population of **Baku** during the interval between the withdrawal of the British expeditionary force and the entry of the Ottoman troops in mid-September. The revenge for the **March Days** was ferocious, and conservative estimates set the number of Armenian lives lost at nine to ten thousand, a figure higher than the total of Muslim losses in all previous outbreaks of intercommunal violence. *See also* DUNSTERVILLE, LIONEL C.

SHAHRIYAR (1906–1988). Pen name of Muhammad Huseyn Hajji Miragoghli, regarded as one of the greatest poets of Iranian Azerbaijan in the 20th century. An accomplished writer in Persian, in the early 1950s he composed his first major work in Azeri, *Haidar Babaya Salam* (Greeting to Haidar Baba). A poetic expression of an Azeri's attachment to his language, homeland, customs, and, not the least, his ethnic identity, it appeared in print in 1954, breaking the long period of the Pahlavi regime's ban on publications in the native language of Azerbaijan. Republished in Soviet Azerbaijan and Turkey, *Haidar Babaya Salam* was recognized as the major poetic work of the year in any Turkic language. Following its publication in Iran, a few other books on Azerbaijani folklore and language appeared in print, some in Persian. *See also* IRANIAN AZERBAIJAN.

SHAHTAKHTINSKI (SHAHTAKHTINLI), MAMMAD AGHA (1846–1931). Journalist, scholar, and political writer. Educated in Germany and France, Shahtakhtinski spent many years in Turkey, where he was a correspondent for the Russian newspaper *Moskovskie vedomosti* (Moscow News). His journalistic activity included the publication in 1903 of the Tbilisi-based newspaper, *Sharq-i rus* (The Russian East), which called for the use of Azeri as the literary language of the Transcaucasian Muslims. This call, which implied emancipation from linguistic influences of Ottoman Turkish, resulted in Shahtakhtinski's being accused of undermining the unity of Turkic peoples in the interest of Russia. In the period of the 1905 Russian Revolution, he was elected deputy to the Second State Duma, but in 1908, the year of the victorious **Young Turkish Revolution,** he moved to Istanbul. He returned to Azerbaijan under the independent republic, taking part in establishing **Baku State University.**

In the early Soviet period he was a motivating force in the preparations for **alphabet reform,** one of the main concerns in his work as a writer and scholar throughout most of his life. *See also* ALPHABET REFORM; AZARIJILAR; PRESS.

SHAMIL (1797–1871). *Imam* (the leader of the Faithful) of the Murid movement, an outgrowth of the Sunni Sufi Naqshbandi order, in **Daghestan** and Chechnya in the first half of the 19th century. After assuming the leadership of the *ghazavat* (holy war) in 1834, Shamil inflicted a series of humiliating defeats upon Russian forces in the Caucasus—numerous expeditions sent against him were unsuccessful. His influence reached northern regions of Azerbaijan, where the inhabitants were responsive to the calls for local uprisings. During the 1840s he had under his command some 20,000 warriors. Only in the late 1850s, with Russia committing large forces, and the mountaineers weakened by internal divisions and exhaustion, did the resistance begin to crumble. Losing popular support, Shamil surrendered in 1859, having delayed the Russian conquest of the Caucasus by a quarter of a century. His place in history became the subject of controversy in the Soviet period: in departure from the earlier view of Shamil as the leader of an anticolonialist people's war, the Stalinist historiography termed him the stooge of Turkey and British imperialism. *See also* CHECHENO-INGUSHETIA; DAGHESTAN.

SHAMKHOR MASSACRE. Following the October 1917 Bolshevik seizure of power in Petrograd, the **Azeris** began to form national military units on the pattern of their Christian neighbors. Lacking other sources of supply, the Azeris began to disarm Russian troops to obtain their weapons. In January 1918 they intercepted a troop train at the Shamkhor station on the Tbilisi-**Baku** rail line. When the troops refused to relinquish their weapons, the Azeris attacked them, causing nearly a thousand deaths. The event aggravated relations between Azeri leaders and the Bolsheviks, leading to confrontations later in the year.

SHAMS AL-DIN ILDIGUZ (1136–1174). Founder of the Ildiguz dynasty. Shams al-Din Ildiguz was a *ghulam* (military slave) of Kipchak origin who rose rapidly in **Seljuk** service. Sultan Mas'ud (1134–1152) married him to Tughril II's widow, making him stepfather to the future sultan. By 1136 he had acquired a power base in Azerbaijan, a major source of Seljuk troops. In 1161 he succeeded in placing his stepson, Arslan Shah (1161–1176), on the throne of the Iraqi sultanate.

As de facto ruler of the Seljuk state, Shams al-Din Ildiguz proved to be a formidable opponent of the expansionist Georgian kingdom. His policies were continued by his son and successor Jahan Pahlawan (1175–1186).

SHAUMIAN, STEPAN G. (1878–1918). Born in 1878 in Tbilisi to **Armenian** parents, Shaumian joined the ranks of the Russian Social-Democratic Workers Party (RSDWP) in 1900, and helped to found the Union of Armenian Social Democrats in 1902 before moving to Germany. He graduated from the University of Berlin in 1905 and returned to Tbilisi later that year, becoming the leader of the Caucasian Union Committee of the RSDWP. Shaumian was the Bolshevik chairman of the Baku Soviet at the time of the October Revolution of 1917. Soon after, in December 1917, Lenin appointed him the special commissar for the **Caucasus.** Shaumian kept contacts with the Armenian **Dashnaksutiun** party, which he saw as a source of support for local Bolshevik goals. He used the intercommunal violence of the **March Days** to eliminate nationalistically minded Azeris from the Baku government. In April 1918 he became the chairman and commissar for foreign affairs in the Baku Sovnarkom. The city and its environs became known as the **Baku Commune,** under the authority of the city soviet that included many Dashnakists. Following the fall of Baku to the Ottoman forces on September 16, 1918, Shaumian and 25 other leaders of the Baku Commune were captured in Krasnovodsk by local socialist revolutionaries and shot on September 20, 1918. *See also* BAKU COMMISSARS; BAKU COMMUNE; MARCH DAYS OF 1918.

SHEKI. A region in northern Azerbaijan, north of the **Kura River.** Sheki was a part of Caucasian Albania from the third to the fifth century. It was captured by the Arabs in 654. In the 14th century Sheki was an independent state ruled by Sidi Ahmed Orlat, a member of the turkicized Mongol tribe of the Orlats. In 1402 the region was allied with Tamerlane in his campaign against the Ottoman sultan Bayazid. From 1444 to 1551 Sheki was ruled by the Kara Keshish Oghli dynasty, and the country flourished through agriculture and the export of silk. It later became a vassal of the **Safavids,** but retained a considerable degree of autonomy. However, it eventually lost its independence after being defeated by the armies of the Iranian Shah Tahmasp I (1524–1576). In the mid-18th century the **Sheki Khanate** grew out of this region. *See also* CAUCASIAN ALBANIA; SHEKI KHANATE.

SHEKI KHANATE. A principality in northern Azerbaijan, which existed from the mid-18th to the early 19th century, centered on the town of Sheki. The khanate was established by Itadji Chelebi-khan. Beginning in the late 18th century, the khans of Sheki sought Russian protection against Iranian reconquest, and in 1805 a treaty was signed that submitted the khanate to Russian overlordship, but the next year there followed a rebellion against Russia. The Russian overlordship was confirmed by the Treaty of Gulistan signed in 1813. The khanate became a Russian province under military administration until it was incorporated into the Caspian oblast in 1840. It later became part of the **Baku** *guberniia* in 1859 and the Elizavetpol *guberniia* in 1868.

SHEMAKHA. One of the oldest towns in Azerbaijan, dating from the sixth century A.D. From the ninth to the 16th centuries, Shemakha was the capital of the **Shirvanshahs.** Its numerous historical buildings have beeen damaged or destroyed by frequent earthquakes, the last major one in 1859. Subsequently, the town was eclipsed by rapidly growing **Baku.** Shemakha is now a center of the food and wine industries, with a population in 1991 of 26,000.

SHIRVAN. A region in northern Azerbaijan, on the western shore of the Caspian Sea. The name "Shirvan" came into use in the Sassanid era (226–651) as a designation for part of ancient **Caucasian Albania,** later known as **Arran.** Shirvan was ruled by a succession of dynasties of **Shirvanshahs** who controlled all the territory from the **Kura River** to **Derbent.** The Shirvan state was originally created by the Sassanids around 600 to defend the frontier against the Khazars. The principal dynasties of **Shirvanshahs** were the Arab **Mazyadids** (ninth–early 11th centuries), the **Kesranids** (11th–14th centuries), and the **Derbent Shirvanshahs** (1382–1538). The state expanded over the centuries to include Derbent, Sheki, and the Mughan steppe south of the **Araxes River**. Its capital was the city of **Shemakha**. The state of the Shirvanshahs became wealthy through trade in oil and salt, and paid an annual tribute of one million dirhams. Shirvan was annexed by the **Safavids,** and became a province of the Safavid state in 1538. It managed to regain its independence from Iran in 1748 and formed the **Shirvan Khanate.** The region was annexed by the Russian Empire in 1805. *See also* ARRAN; DERBENT SHIRVANSHAHS; KESRANIDS; MAZYADIDS; SHIRVAN KHANATE; SHIRVANSHAHS.

SHIRVAN KHANATE. A principality in northern Azerbaijan which was centered on the region of **Shirvan.** The khanate was formed after it was liberated from the domination of the Iranian ruler Nadir Shah in 1748. It was one of the wealthiest khanates in northern Azerbaijan specializing in agriculture and the export of silk and other fabrics. To avoid Iranian reconquest the khanate was incorporated into the Russian Empire in 1805. This annexation was confirmed by the Treaty of **Gulistan** in 1813. In 1820 the khanate's government was abolished and replaced with a Russian military administration. It was made a *provintsiia* of Russia and in 1840 became part of the Caspian *oblast*. In 1849 it was included in the **Baku** *guberniia*. *See also* SHIRVAN.

SHIRVANI, SAYYID, AZIM (1835–1888). A leading **Azeri** poet and educator of the period of intellectual change brought by the early impact of Europe. Although Shirvani's education was thoroughly traditional, including studies in Arab countries, his poetry expressed reformist concerns of the rising Azeri **intelligentsia.** He was an ardent supporter of the first Azeri language newspaper, *Akinchi,* and in 1869 founded in his native town of Shemakha the first modernized (**Jadidist**) school in Azerbaijan. *See also* JADIDISM.

SHIRVANSHAHS. The rulers of the state of **Shirvan** in northern Azerbaijan from the sixth to the 16th centuries. The Shirvan state was created by the Sassanids to defend their Caucasian frontier against the Khazars. It contained the lands from the **Kura River** to the town of **Derbent,** and had its capital at the city of Shemakha. The ruling dynasties of the Shirvanshahs were: the **Mazyadids** (ninth–11th centuries), the **Kesranids** (11th–14th centuries), and the **Derbent Shirvanshahs** (1382–1538). The state of the Shirvanshahs was annexed by the **Safavid** ruler Tahmasp I (1524–1576) in 1538. The last Shirvanshah, Shanrukh, was captured and taken to **Tabriz** where he was executed. *See also* DERBENT SHIRVANSHAHS; KESRANIDS; MAZYADIDS; SHIRVAN.

SILK ROAD. The name of an ancient caravan route linking the Far East with the Western world. The main product carried westward was silk. The route originated in central China, and passed through territories of Central Asia and part of the Middle East, including **Tabriz,** to end up at the Mediterranean coast. The Silk Road and its branches was for centuries the economic lifeline of the regions it traversed.

Its use declined with the waning of Roman power in the Middle East and the rise of Arab conquests. There followed a revival under the Mongols in the 13th and 14th centuries, which in turn was followed by another decline with the development of maritime commerce in the 15th century. The most recent attempt at reinvigorating the ancient East–West trade route has been the Europe–Caucasus–Asia Transport Corridor known under the acronym TRACEA and sometimes called the New Silk Road . In the summer of 1998, twelve nations in the regions of Caucasia, the Black Sea, and Central Asia reached an agreement to develop rail, road, air, and sea links from China and Mongolia to Europe. The agreement provides for regulating transport, tariffs, and custom procedures as well as setting up a permanent secretariat in **Baku.** The planned route would offer the newly independent states access to Western markets, while bypassing the territory of Russia.

A nonregional power, the United States, lent its support with the Silk Road Strategy Acts of 1997 and 1998. These acts provide for strengthened independence of the region's countries; solution of their conflicts; development of free market economies; and commitment to democracy, freedom, and human rights.

SOVEREIGNITY LAW. The Sovereignity Law was drafted on September 25, 1989, by the Supreme Soviet of the **Azerbaijani Soviet Socialist Republic** following the wave of strikes that shook Azerbaijan in 1989, in itself a sign of the Soviet regime's decline. The law accepted the jurisdiction of the USSR's laws only when they did not violate the sovereign rights of the Azerbaijani SSR. It reaffirmed Azerbaijan's jurisdiction over Nagorno-Karabagh and Nakhichevan and stipulated that the frontiers of the Republic could not be changed without the approval of the Azerbaijani nation. The law included a provision for the right of Azerbaijan to secede from the USSR after a referendum of the entire population of the Republic. The Sovereignity Law was rejected by Moscow on the grounds that it contradicted the USSR's constitution, which gave the right of legislating to the Supreme Soviet of the USSR.

-T-

TABRIZ. The largest city of **Iranian Azerbaijan,** and the capital of the Eastern Azerbaijani *ostan* (province). Tabriz is an important industrial center and the junction of highways and railroads serving Iran's trade with Russia and Turkey.

Founded in the fourth century under the Sassanid dynasty, between the late 13th century and early 16th century Tabriz functioned as the capital of various states that emerged on the territory of present-day Iran, including the early period of the **Safavid** kingdom. In the 18th century, Tabriz became the capital of the khanate bearing the same name, and under the **Qajar** dynasty it was the official residence of the crown princes of Iran. As the second city in the kingdom, it was in many ways the rival of Teheran. Through its commercial contacts with Turkey and Russia, as well as through extensive labor migrations to **Caucasia,** Tabriz was receptive to political stirrings from across the border, and these accounted for its special role in the **Iranian Constitutional Revolution** of 1906–1911. The city rebelled against Shah Muhammad Ali, and his forces laid siege on Tabriz for six months until April 1909.

After the demise of the Iranian revolution, Tabriz was occupied by Russian forces until the overthrow of the tsardom in 1917. Subsequently, the city became the center of the reformist movement headed by Shaikh Muhammad **Khiabani,** whose aim was to gain autonomy from the central government. Khiabani's uprising was suppressed by the Teheran government in September 1920, but two years later Tabriz witnessed another brief rebellion, led by the gendarme officer Abu'l Qasim Lahuti.

Under the regime of the Pahlavi dynasty, the policy of centralizing commerce in Iran's capital dealt a heavy blow to Tabriz. The city lost its commercial supremacy, and its most active inhabitants moved to Teheran. During **World War II** it was occupied by Red Army forces, and under the Soviet-backed autonomist regime of the **Democratic Party of Azerbaijan** it became the center of activities for the revival of **Azeri** culture and education. Tabriz lost this position after returning under the authority of the central government of Iran in late 1946. It shared in the economic expansion of the late Pahlavi period, when it became an important industrial center, with the population reaching 600,000 by 1976. In 1978 Tabriz was in the forefront of the protest movement, which, within a year, led to the overthrow of the monarchy in Iran. Under the Islamic Republic, Tabriz was once again the scene of mass protest against Teheran because of overcentralization resulting from the new constitution of Iran. *See also* AZADISTAN; AZERBAIJAN; IRANIAN.

TAGHIYEV, HAJI ZEYNAL ABDIN (1838–1924). An **Azeri** entrepreneur and philanthropist reputed to have been the richest man in **Transcaucasia.** Beginning with highly successful investments in the **oil industry,** he branched out into extensive land and stock market speculations. Himself lacking in education, Taghiyev financially supported a wide range of educational ventures, among them schools, scholarships, theater, and newspapers—including *Hayat* (Life) and *Fuyuzat* (Abundance) in Azeri, and *Kaspii* (The Caspian) in Russian. His generosity benefited Azerbaijan as well as Iran and Muslim centers of Russia. In Russian Azerbaijan, Taghiyev's backing became an important factor in the native cultural revival. *See also* EDUCATION; PRESS.

TALYSH KHANATE. A principality established by Sayyid Abbas, in the mid-18th century on the southwest coast of the Caspian Sea. The capital was the town of Lenkoran.

The khanate became a protectorate in 1802, and was finally annexed by Russia in 1828 under the terms of the **Treaty of Turkmanchai.** *See also* TALYSHIS.

TALYSH MOUNTAINS. A mountain range in southeastern Azerbaijan on the border with Iran. It is a continuation of the Lesser Caucasus Range, but is separated by the **Araxes River** valley. Its highest point is Mt. Kiumiurkei at 7,440 feet (2,477 m).

TALYSHIS. An ethnic group inhabiting the southeastern border area of Azerbaijan and northern Iran, estimated at 250,000. Members speak a language (Talyshi) that belongs to the northwestern group of Iranian languages and has several dialects. Almost all of the Talyshis living in Azerbaijan speak **Azeri** as well, which is their literary language. They are predominantly Shi'ite in religion. Today the Talyshis have largely been assimilated into the Azeri population. In the post-Soviet period the Talysh People's Party headed by Ali Akram Gumbatov raised demands for autonomy and federal restructuring of the **Republic of Azerbaijan.** In support of its claims, the party began to organize armed squads. It ceased its activities after Haidar **Aliyev** came to power, and Gambatov joined the Azeri émigré politicians in Moscow. *See also* TALYSH KHANATE.

TATAR-ARMENIAN WAR. The name given by the world press to the interethnic violence that raged in **Transcaucasia** during the Russian Revolution of the years 1905–1907.

Armenian-Azeri antagonism had grown into a multifaceted problem. In addition to its cultural–religious dimension, it involved such factors as grievances of the fledgling Azeri entrepreneurial class beset by ruinous competition, the conflict of interests between unskilled Muslim laborers and Armenian entrepreneurs and merchants, and the animosity of the predominantly rural Azeris toward the more urbanized Armenians.

The differences in social structure of the two communities found their parallel in the degree to which each was politically organized. In contrast to the Azeris, the Armenians had produced a dynamic nationalist movement spearheaded by the **Dashnaktsutiun.** The party's avowed objective was the creation of a free and autonomous Armenian state in the Ottoman provinces of eastern Anatolia, and it saw its enemy in the Turkey of Abdul Hamid II. Yet, at the turn of the century, Armenian nationalism found itself on a collision course with the assimilationist drive of the tsarist regime. On their part, the Russian authorities in Transcaucasia, in a temporary reversal of their traditional policies, made some gestures aimed at winning over the Muslims. The measure of direct responsibility borne by the tsarist officials for the events that followed has not been fully determined, and at any rate there was enough accumulated hostility between the two peoples to itself provoke the conflict without outside prodding.

The first outbreaks of Muslim-Armenian violence occurred in **Baku** on February 6, 1905, resulting in three days of killing and looting while the police and troops remained conspicuously inactive, as they would be during most of the clashes to come.

The horrors of Baku recurred, on a smaller scale, in **Erivan** on February 20–21, then in May in **Nakhichevan** and other parts of the Erivan *guberniia,* and in early June in Shusha. Another wave of violence swept Baku toward the end of August with an even more destructive fury than in February, and some Armenian-owned oil fields were set on fire. At the end of September the town of Kazakh was burned down in the course of rioting. One of the bloodiest clashes took place in **Ganja** on November 15–18, and there was another in Tbilisi on November 21. The fighting continued well into the next year, though with lesser intensity.

The hostilities were not confined to the towns: an estimated 128 to 158 Muslim villages were pillaged or destroyed. The estimates of lives lost vary widely, ranging from 3,100 to 10,000, but all of the available data indicate that the Muslims suffered greater losses.

The blows suffered at the hands of the Dashnakist squads became a catalyst for the consolidation of the Muslim community of Azerbaijan. The "Tatar-Armenian War" generated for the first time solidarity among Muslims in a cause transcending local, sectarian, or kinship loyalties, and such divisions ceased to be an impediment to political action. The symbol of unity was still the green banner of the Prophet, but the religious appeal functioned mainly as a traditional means of mobilizing the population for an ethnic conflict. Although the cries "Death to the Infidel" were heard, the slogan was in reference to the Armenians, and excluded Georgians, Russians, and other Christians.

The pro-Muslim posture of the tsarist authorities did not last beyond the initial stage of the fighting: in May 1905 Russian troops were under orders to fire at the "Tatars." This new Russian about-face came with the appointment of Vorontsov-Dashkov as viceroy of the Caucasus. While cultivating an image of benevolence toward all the inhabitants of the region, he considered Armenians as a people attached to property, family, and religion, and as such natural supporters of law and stability. Moreover, among the high-ranking tsarist officials, he belonged to the partisans of renewed expansion in the Middle East, in which he saw the Armenians again playing the part of Russia's "advance guard." *See also* ARMENIANS IN AZERBAIJAN; DIFAI; VORONTSOV-DASHKOV.

THEATER, AZERI. Azeri theater had its beginnings in the ancient folk festivals and dances of the Azeri people. The earliest theater in Azerbaijan may have been the puppet shows called *Kilim arasi* (Behind the Carpet), which parodied social injustice. *Tamasha* (folk theater) were popular pastimes with short satirical or comic sketches. In the Medieval period, religious mystery theater became quite popular and reflected the values of traditional Azerbaijani society.

Theater in a European sense appeared in Azerbaijan only with the rise of modern literature in the mid-19th century. Drama was the favorite literary form of Mirza Fath Ali **Akhundzade,** whose satires written in the native language earned him the reputation of the "Moliére of the Orient." The first performances of Akhundzade's comedies, *Haji Qara* (Adventures of a Miser) and *Vizier of the Lenkoran Khanate* were both presented in **Baku** in 1873. In the view of the modernizers, theater was an especially suitable medium of communication for spreading the ideas of the enlightenment to a broad public that was largely illiterate. Azerbaijan gained the distinction of being a pioneer of theater in the Turkic world as well as in Iran. While Akhundzade wrote comedies satirizing what he perceived as social ills, his immediate successors Najaf bey **Vazirov** and Abdul Rahman Haqverdiyev introduced the genre of tragedy, reflecting the sense of isolation of the **intelligentsia** from the society of the time.

The years between the two Russian Revolutions, 1905–1917, saw the consolidation of theatrical life around educational or charitable institutions such as in the plays *Nijat* (Salvation), and *Safa* (Purity), as well as the transition toward professionalism on the part of actors and directors. The same period of cultural upsurge witnessed the first Azeri opera,

Layla and Majnun (1908), based on the 16th-century poem of the same name by **Fuzuli** and set to the music of Uzeir **Hajibeyli** (1885–1948).

With the coming of Soviet power, all theaters were nationalized and their repertories were strictly supervised by the authorities. On the other hand, the performing arts benefited from the steady financial support of the state. In 1924 the Theater of Opera and Ballet was founded in Baku. Despite the increasing pressure of official guidance and controls, which reached their peak under Stalin, plays remained a favorite literary form of many writers. During **World War II** plays glorifying the soldier at the front and historic subjects depicting Azerbaijan's wars against foreign (non-Russian) invaders were common.

The post-war period witnessed productions that reflected problems of morality and ethics in the education of the young. Works such as *Eye Doctor* by I. Safarli, *The Bumpkin* by Mirza Ibrahimov, and *You Are Always With Me* by Ilyas Efendiyev illustrated the experiences of modern Soviet life. This was generally a period of stagnation of Azeri theater, a condition began that to improve with the introduction of glasnost in the 1980s. With the separation from Moscow in 1991, Azeris began rediscovering national cultural themes. *See also* INTELLIGENTSIA; LITERATURE.

TOPCHIBASHI (TOPCHIBASHEV), ALI MARDAN BEY (1869–1934). A lawyer by profession and prominent figure of Azerbaijani politics of the early 20th century. He began his public life as the editor in chief of the Azeri-owned Russian language newspaper *Kaspii* (The Caspian). Topchibashi campaigned for the improvement of Muslim **education,** access for Muslims to positions in the Russian civil service, and alleviation of the peasants' poverty. In August 1905 he was a delegate to the First All-Russian Muslim Congress at Nizhni Novgorod. He was the chairman of the Second All-Russian Muslim Congress in St. Petersburg in January 1906 at which he was elected to the central committee of the **Ittifaq** Party. Under the **Azerbaijani Democratic Republic,** he became the president of the Parliament, a position equivalent to that of head of state, and in this capacity went to the Paris Peace Conference at Versailles to seek recognition of Azerbaijan's independence. Following the Bolshevik overthrow of the Azerbaijani Democratic Republic, Topchibashi remained in exile in Paris, active in émigré political life. *See also* AZERBAIJANI DEMOCRATIC REPUBLIC; *KASPII*.

TRANSCAUCASIA. The name used in Russia and Europe for the region that lies south of the **Caucasus** mountain range. It comprises the countries of Azerbaijan, Armenia, and Georgia, and extends south of the Greater Caucasus. The region includes the southern slopes of the Greater Caucasus, the Colchis Lowland, the Kura Depression, the Lesser Caucasus, the Dzhavakhet-Armenian Plateau, and the **Talysh Mountains** with the Lenkoran Lowland. It is bordered in the north by the Russian Republic, in the east by the **Caspian Sea,** and in the west by the Black Sea. In the south it is bordered by the Lower Caucasus Range and by Turkey and Iran.

TRANSCAUCASIAN COMMISSARIAT (ZAKAVKOM). The Transcaucasian Commissariat was the successor of the **Ozakom** and was formed in Tbilisi after the Bolshevik seizure of power in Petrograd, on November 28, 1917. The Commissariat consisted of 12 members from various Transcaucasian political organizations such as the Mensheviks, Socialist Revolutionaries, Dashnakists, and Musavatists. The Zakavkom sought separation of **Transcaucasia** from Bolshevik-run Russia. In pursuance of this policy it concluded treaties with the anti-Bolshevi Kuban *Rada* and the White Guard Ataman A. M. Kaledin, and with the leaders of **Daghestan** and Terek. In November and December 1917 the Commissariat ordered the suppression of Bolshevik newspapers, the seizure of the arsenal in Tbilisi, and the disarming of pro-Bolshevik troops. On February 23, 1918, it created the **Transcaucasian Seim** to oversee the secession of Transcaucasia from Soviet Russia. On March 26, 1918, the Transcaucasian Seim dissolved the **Transcaucasian Commissariat** after Armenia, Azerbaijan, and Georgia declared themselves independent republics. *See also* OZAKOM; TRANSCAUCASIAN SEIM.

TRANSCAUCASIAN FEDERATION. An independent state made up of Armenia, Azerbaijan, and Georgia, which declared its independence from Russia on April 22, 1918, and lasted until May 26, 1918. The Federation was proclaimed by the **Transcaucasian Seim** as a condition for signing the peace treaty with the Ottoman state, negotiated at the **Trebizond Peace Talks,** and the government under Georgian Menshevik Akakii Ckhenkeli was formed in Tbilisi. On May 26, 1918, Georgia, encouraged by Germany, withdrew from the Federation and declared its independence. Armenia and Azerbaijan followed suit on May 28, putting an end to the Transcaucasian Federation. *See also* TRANSCAUCASIAN SEIM.

TRANSCAUCASIAN SEIM (DIET). A regional legislative body convened by the Transcaucasian Commissariat in Tbilisi on February 10, 1918, as the supreme locus of power over Transcaucasia after the dispersal of the Constituent Assembly of Russia by the Bolsheviks. The membership of the Seim was determined by lowering the minimum number of votes to one-third of that which had been required for a seat in the Constituent Assembly. On the basis of this formula, the larger parties tripled the number of their deputies and the minor ones obtained representation that voters had previously denied. The largest parliamentary groups were the Georgian Mensheviks, Musavatists, and Dashnakists. The Bolsheviks protested against the creation of the Seim and refused to participate. In March 1918, the Seim voted on the formal secession of Transcaucasia from Soviet Russia, and on April 22, 1918, proclaimed Transcaucasia an independent federal republic. Four weeks later, with Georgia withdrawing from the Federation, the Seim dissolved itself on May 26, 1918. *See also* TRANSCAUCASIAN COMMISSARIAT; TRANSCAUCASIAN FEDERATION.

TRANSCAUCASIAN SOVIET FEDERATED SOCIALIST REPUBLIC (ZAKFEDERATSIIA). A regional group of Soviet republics that brought together Georgia, Armenia, and Azerbaijan into one subdivision of the USSR from 1922 to 1936. The *Zakfederatsiia* was formed with the aim of rebuilding **Transcaucasia** after the disruptions of the civil war period, and to combat the nationalist sentiments of its peoples. On March 12, 1922, a conference of representatives of the Central Executive Committee of the soviets from the three republics convened in Tbilisi to approve a treaty on formation of the Transcaucasian Soviet Federated Republic. On December 30, 1922, the Zakfederatsiia joined the Russian, Ukrainian, and Byelorussian Soviet republics to form the USSR. The Zakfederatsiia remained in existence until 1936, when the new Stalin Constitution of the USSR made Azerbaijan, Georgia, and Armenia constituent republics of the USSR. The federation was dissolved among hints that the idea of the regional association smacked of the counterrevolutionary 1918 **Transcaucasian Federation.** From that point on, only vertical relations with the center would be allowed, rather than horizontal links among the national republics, a prelude to the process of forging a new Soviet nation.

TREBIZOND PEACE TALKS (1918). A peace conference between the **Transcaucasian Seim** and the Ottoman state, which was held in the Turkish town of Trebizond from March 12, 1918, to April 13, 1918. The purpose of the talks was to end **Transcaucasia's** participation in **World War I.** The Seim wanted a return to the 1914 international boundaries and self-determination for eastern Anatolia. The Ottoman delegation wanted the acceptance by the Seim of the Treaty of Brest-Litovsk, which called for the cession of Batum, Kars, and Ardahan as well as Transcaucasian territories occupied by Ottoman Turkey since the commencement of hostilities. The **Armenians** and Georgians were opposed to accepting this condition, but the **Azeris** were willing to accept it since the lands in question were not theirs and this fit nicely with the Pan-Turkic sentiment to be found among the Azeri people. The non-Muslim majority of the Seim voted for war against the Ottoman Empire on April 13, and the peace delegation was recalled to Tbilisi the next day.

In response, the Ottoman Army advanced and took Batum, but was stopped at Kars. On April 22, the Ottomans and the Seim agreed to cease fighting and resume the peace talks. Under pressure from the Ottoman Turks, the Scim declared Transcaucasia an independent, democratic, federal republic on April 22, 1918, which would be known as the **Transcaucasian Federation.** On May 11, the talks resumed in Batum. *See also* TRANSCAUCASIAN FEDERATION; TRANSCAUCASIAN SEIM.

TURKIC PARTY OF DECENTRALIZATION (TURK ADAM-I MARKAZIYYAT FIRQASI). Also known as the Federalist Party, it was formed in **Ganja** in the spring of 1917 by Nasib bey **Yusufbayli,** and other political figures of Ganja who in the past had links with the **Difai** party. The Adam-i Markaziyyat advocated the restructuring of the Russian Empire into a federation of autonomous units to safeguard the free development of their national components. Although t he leadership included some large landowners, the party enjoyed a wide popular following in Ganja province due to its support of Azeri national identity. On June 20, 1917, the Adam-i Markaziyyat merged with the **Musavat Party,** creating the Turkic Party of Federalists— **Musavat** (*Turk Adam-i Markaziyyat—Musavat Firqasi). See also* MUSAVAT; YUSUFBEYLI, NASIB BEY.

TURKMANCHAI, TREATY OF (1828). Treaty ending the Second **Russo-Iranian War** of 1826–1828. It was signed in the village of Turkmanchai on February 10, 1828. Under the terms of the Treaty,

Russia received the eastern Azerbaijani Khanates of **Erivan** and **Nakhichevan,** Iran pledged not to interfere with the resettlement of Armenians in Russia, and agreed to pay reparations of 20 million rubles in silver. In addition, Russia's exclusive right to maintain a **Caspian Sea** fleet was affirmed, and capitulatory rights guaranteed Russia preferential treatment for its exports, which generally were not competitive in European markets. The Treaty of Turkmanchai was the definitive acknowledgment of the Iranian loss of the **Caucasus** region to Russia and of the permanent division of the **Azeri** people. *See also* GULISTAN, TREATY OF (1813); RUSSO-IRANIAN WAR, FIRST (1804–1813); RUSSO-IRANIAN WAR, SECOND (1826–1828).

-V-

VAZIROV, ABDUL RAKHMAN. First secretary of the **Communist Party of Azerbaijan** in the period of its final decline, 1988–1990. Vazirov, formerly Soviet ambassador to Pakistan, replaced Kamran **Baghirov** as party head in May 1988. Faced with the **Nagorno-Karabagh dispute,** emergence of "informal" associations, and growing restiveness of the population, Vazirov's rule was insecure from the beginning. In July and August 1989 the **People's Front of Azerbaijan** (PFAz) launched a series of demonstrations and strikes forcing him to concessions. Early in January 1990 the PFAz seized the town of Lenkoran and began removing the frontier installations between Azerbaijan and Iran. By mid-month the events of **Black January** in Baku took place, with anti-Armenian violence and the subsequent intervention of the Soviet Army. Blamed for indecisiveness and poor leadership, Vazirov was forced from office. His successor, the last first secretary, was Ayaz Niyazi **Mutalibov.** *See also* BLACK JANUARY 1990; PEOPLE'S FRONT OF AZERBAIJAN (PFAz).

VAZIROV, NAJAF BEY (1854–1926). A member of the *Akinchi* circle of writers who subsequently became a prominent playwright and the first of the successors to Mirza Fath Ali **Akhundzade**'s mantle. Apart from writing satirical comedies, he was the author of the first **Azeri** tragedies. This innovation is seen as the reflection of conflict between change and tradition reaching an intensity that resulted in personal situations of tragic dimensions. Vazirov's characters were often individuals striving to reform the old ways who were crushed by the tradition-bound conservative environment. They expressed the sense of isolation experienced by the members of the **intelligentsia** of his day. *See also* AZERI; PRESS; THEATER.

VORONTSOV, MIKHAIL, PRINCE (1782–1856). One of Russia's most able 19th-century statesmen and administrators. Born and raised in England, he developed liberal inclinations and an appreciation for the rule of law. He served as an army officer during the Napoleonic Wars and was the commander of the occupation forces in France. In 1823 he was appointed the governor-general of New Russia—southern Ukraine where he remained for 30 years. In recognition of his work, Nicholas I appointed him the viceroy of the Caucasus in 1845, reporting directly to the tsar. Vorontsov's policies toward the Muslims of **Transcaucasia** aimed at winning over their "privileged estates" by guaranteeing their property rights, and opening doors for careers in government service. He lent his support to the **Azeri** literary renaissance and among his beneficiaries was Mirza Fath Ali **Akhundzade**. *See also* DECEMBER RESCRIPT.

VORONTSOV-DASHKOV, ILLARION, COUNT (1837–1916). Russian statesman and army officer, who held various posts at the court and in the central government. In 1905 he was appointed to the restored position of the viceroy of the Caucasus with the task of dealing with the revolutionary situation in the region. His policy consisted of alternating between firmness and conciliatory gestures. A believer in Russia's need to expand into the Middle East, he tended to favor **Armenians** at the expense of the **Azeris**. *See also* TATAR-ARMENIAN WAR.

-W-

WORLD WAR I AND AZERBAIJAN. The outbreak of the First World War initially had little impact upon Azerbaijan, until three months later when Turkey declared war against Russia at the end of October in 1914. The **Azeris** were exempt from conscription, as were all Muslims of Russia, although they could serve as volunteers or professional soldiers.

Azerbaijan figured highly in Turkey's war plans as the stepping stone to the future state uniting the Ottoman Turks with the Turks of

Caucasia and even Central Asia. The immediate objective of the Ottoman war minister Enver Pasha, was to destroy the bulk of the Russian forces between Kars and Sarikamish, after which would follow the conquest of **Transcaucasia.** Enver's Caucasian offensive ended in disaster, with the Ottoman Third Army losing 85 percent of its strength. From the winter of 1915 on, the strategic initiative on the Caucasus front was in the Russian hands. In 1915, the Armenians behind Ottoman lines suffered mass deportations and killings. After an extended lull, the Russians, who had been unable to come to their rescue, captured the fortress of Erzerum in February of the next year. In July 1916, the Russian army reached its farthest point of advance in Anatolia, Erzincan.

A secondary theater of operations was **Iranian Azerbaijan,** which served as a corridor for flanking or diversionary movements aimed at **Baku.** In the first three years of the war, the Ottoman actions from Anatolia or Mesopotamia did not, however, exceed the scale of brief forays.

Unlike Iran's **Tabriz** province, Russian Azerbaijan remained far from military operations for most of the war. Here, the attitudes reflected changing fortunes of the Russo–Ottoman conflict. As the fighting in the Caucasus front began to favor Russia, the Azeri elites gladly responded to the tsardom's attempts at improving mutual relations. The new approach was marked by the appointment in the fall of 1915 of Grand Duke Nicholas Nicholaevich as the viceroy of the Caucasus. The improved atmosphere coincided with the recovery of oil prices, after a steep decline at the outset of the war because of the threat to Black Sea shipping. The threat receded with the Russian successes on the **Caucasus** front, and the year 1915 brought another series of impressive victories. In a display of psychological adaptation, Azerbaijani clergymen held prayers on the occasion of the Russian seizure of Erzerum. Ottoman fortunes were not destined for restoration until the Russian Revolution of 1917 created an entirely new situation behind the front, and then on the front itself.

Among the consequences of the disintegration of the Russian Caucasus front was the resurgence of Turanian designs, now that the Ottoman troops were facing denuded enemy positions. As in 1914, in the spring and summer of 1918 these designs were predicated on achieving two interlinked goals, which at last appeared to be within the realm of possibility: the conquest of Baku and the extension of an Ottoman military presence over both Azerbaijans.

Tabriz province, together with its capital, passed under Ottoman occupation during the summer months, and another force that included Azeri irregulars organized into the **Army of Islam,** seized Baku in mid-September—on behalf of the **Azerbaijani Democratic Republic.**

Turkey's moment of glory in both Azerbaijans came when the Ottoman State was near the final stage of war fatigue. By the end of October, an armistice agreement was signed with the Allies in Mudros (Greece). The Ottoman troops had to withdraw from Transcaucasia, which would be occupied by British forces. *See also* ARMY OF ISLAM; AZERBAIJANI DEMOCRATIC REPUBLIC.

WORLD WAR II AND AZERBAIJAN. During the Second World War, Azerbaijan attracted special attention from all sides involved in the region. In the first phase of the war the British and French considered bombing the **Baku** oil fields from air bases in Syria and Iraq, to stop Soviet supplies flowing to Germany. When the Germans invaded the USSR, their war aims called for the seizure of **Transcaucasia** to acquire the oil necessary to pursuing the war effort. The **Caspian** oil deposits were the objective of the main offensive of the year 1942, which brought the German troops to the **Caucasus** mountain range, including Elbruz peak, but not beyond. For the Soviets, Azerbaijan became a major weapons and fuel producing center as well as a source of manpower. During the war, Azerbaijan delivered 75 million tons of oil and 22 million tons of gasoline and oil products. By 1942, 45,000 **Azeris** were serving in Soviet armies, with many more conscripted during the course of the war. Soviet propaganda of the period emphasized Azerbaijan's historic battles against foreign (non-Russian) invaders and glorified soldiers at the front. As many as 30,000 Azeris were decorated for bravery during the course of the war. On the other hand, at least 35,000 Azeris out of some 110,000 natives of **Caucasia** were fighting on the German side in 1943 alone. Some had volunteered for German-formed units to escape starvation and overwork in the German prisoner of war camps. Many others joined because of anti-Soviet sentiment. A large number of these men were imprisoned or executed following their repatriation after the war. Soviet victory against Germany assured that Azerbaijan remained firmly under the USSR's control. *See also* IRANIAN AZERBAIJAN; OIL INDUSTRY.

-Y-

YENI KAFKASIYYE **(NEW CAUCASIA).** A Turkish-language journal of the **Azeri** émigrés from the Soviet regime, published in Istanbul in the years 1923–1927. *Yeni Kafkasiyye* purported to speak for all of the nationalities of Caucasia and promoted the ideas of independence from Russia and regional federalism.

YOUNG TURKISH REVOLUTION (1908). In contrast to the recent revolutions in Russia and Iran, the overthrow of the absolutist regime of Abdul Hamid II in Turkey by a military coup was swift and permanent. On July 24, 1908, the Ottoman constitution was restored, and the dominant force became the Committee of Union and Progress (CUP), a part of the former opposition broadly defined as the Young Turkish movement.

Under the new liberal regime, the Ottoman apostles of **Pan-Turkism** found freedom for their activities, including pursuit of their concerns for ethnic cousins abroad. In December 1908 the first association devoted to promoting the ideas of Turkic identity and solidarity, Turk Dernegi (Turkic Circle) was established. Turkic communities from Russia were encouraged to participate, and soon their representatives made their appearance on the Bosporus.

The **Azeri** contingent was particularly strong, as the luminaries of the intellectual elite were moving to Turkey, now the land of promise for their political inclinations or literary ambitions. Their number included such names as Ahmad **Aghayev,** Ali **Huseynzade,** Nasib **Yusufbeyli,** Karabey **Karabeykov, Huseyn Javid,** and after his expulsion from Iran, Mammad Amin **Rasulzade.**

While Aghayev and Huseynzade linked their political fortunes with the cause of Turkey, other Azeris chose, in time, to return home. Some were to disclose a feeling of superiority toward the contemporary Ottoman civilization. Yet for all of their reservations, Azeri intellectuals in general became committed to the ideas of Turkism, which after 1908 had grown into the dominant current in Azerbaijani political thinking. *See also* INTELLIGENTSIA; PAN-TURKISM.

YUSUFBEYLI (USSUBEKOW), NASIB BEY (1881–1920). Native of **Ganja,** he studied at Odessa University, and in 1905 became a founding member of the Ganja-based **Difai** (Defense) party. After the

1905–1907 Russian Revolution, Yusufbayli lived in Bakhchisaray, Crimea, where he worked with Ismail **Gaspirali** in publishing the newspaper *Tarjuman,* and married Gaspirali's daughter, Shafiqa. Following the **Young Turkish Revolution** of 1908, he moved to Istanbul, returning to Ganja the next year. After the overthrow of Tsardom in Russia in 1917, he became one of the founders of the **Turkic Party of Decentralization,** known also as the Federalists. In the fall of 1917, the Ganja Federalists merged with the **Baku**-based **Musavat Party,** forming the Right wing within the united party.

In April 1919 Yusufbeyli became the prime minister of independent Azerbaijan, and in December of the same year he formed his second cabinet. By this time he had shifted his allegiance from the Right to the Left wing of the Musavat. His coalition government was forced to resign on April 1, 1920, because of the withdrawal of support from the Socialist parliamentary group. Following the entry of the Red Army into Azerbaijan, he was killed in early May 1920, during an attempt to find refuge in Georgia. *See also* AZERBAIJANI DEMOCRATIC REPUBLIC; MUSAVAT.

-Z-

ZAKAVKOM. *See* TRANSCAUCASIAN COMMISSARIAT.

ZAKFEDERATSIIA. *See* TRANSCAUCASIAN SOVIET FEDERATED SOCIALIST REPUBLIC.

ZANGEZUR. A strip of land belonging to the Republic of Armenia, which separates the Nakhichevan region from the rest of Azerbaijan. Although originally part of Azerbaijan, it was transferred to Armenia under the arrangements delineating the borders between the Soviet republics of Armenia and Azerbaijan. Moscow's intention in awarding Zangezur to Armenia was to bar free access between Turkey and the bulk of Azerbaijan. *See also* NAKHICHEVAN AUTONOMOUS SOVIET SOCIALIST REPUBLIC.

ZARDABI, HASAN BEY (1832–1907). A **Baku** high school teacher, who became one of the leading figures of the **Azeri** cultural renaissance in the second half of the 19th century. In 1875 he founded the first Turkic language newspaper in the Russian Empire, *Akinchi*

(Ploughman), which became the forum for the Azeri **intelligentsia.**
The newspaper's title reflected Zardabi's populist disposition, which
he acquired in his younger years spent at the University of Moscow
among the followers of the Russian Narodnik movement. In keeping
with the ideas of populism, he promoted the use of native vernacular
as the literary idiom of Azerbaijan instead of Persian. Because of Zardabi's political inclinations, which, strengthened by his affiliation to the
Sunni branch of Islam, included sympathy for Turkey, *Akinchi* was ordered to close down in 1877 during the Russo-Ottoman war. Zardabi
resumed journalistic work in the spirit of the native enlightenment
movement in other press publications, including the Russian-language
newspaper, *Kaspii. See also AKINCHI;* PRESS.

Bibliography

Handbooks, Dictionaries, Bibliographies, Indexes

Armenia, Azerbaijan, and Georgia: Country Studies. Edited by Glenn E. Curtis. Washington, D.C.: Federal Research Service, Library of Congress, 1995.

Atabaki, Touraj. *Baku Documents: Union Catalogue of Persian, Azerbaijani, Ottoman Turkish and Arabic Serials and Newspapers in the Libraries in the Republic of Azerbaijan*. New York: Taurus Academic Studies, 1995.

Azerbaijan Yearbook 1994. Edited by Akif Abdullayev, et al. Baku: Centre for Strategic and International Studies, 1995.

Kuliev, S. M. *English-Azerbaijan-Russian Dictionary on Oil Field Industry*. 2nd edition. Baku: Vahid Aziz, 1995.

Murphy, John D. *Azerbaijani Newspaper Reader*. Kensington, Md.: Dunwoody Press, 1993.

O'Sullivan, Patrick A. *Azerbaijani-English Dictionary*. Kensington, Md.: Dunwoody Press, 1994.

Volozov, Valeriy B. *Azerbaijani Texts with Parallel English Translations*. Kensington, Md.: Dunwoody Press, 1995.

Periodicals

Annual of the Society for the Study of Caucasia. Chicago: The Society for the Study of Caucasia, 1989–. Annual.

Azerbaijan. Washington, D.C.: International Monetary Fund, 1992–. Annual.

Azerbaijan International. Sherman Oaks, Calif.: Azerbaijan International, 1993–. Quarterly.

Caspian Crossroads. Washington, D.C.: U.S.-Azerbaijan Council. 1995–. Quarterly.

Caucasus and the Caspian: Seminar Series. Cambridge, Mass.: Strengthening Democratic Institutions Project, John F. Kennedy School of Government, Harvard University, 1996–. Annual.
Country Profile: Azerbaijan. London: Economist Intelligence Unit, 1991–. Annual.
Journal of Central Asia and Caucasian Review. Teheran: Center for Central Asia and Caucasia Research, Institute for Political and International Studies, 1993–.
Reform. Bethesda, Md.: U.S.A. & Azerbaijan Friendship and Cultural Association, 1995–. Quarterly.

Architecture, Film, Literature, Music

Arif, Mammad. *Literature of the Azerbaijani People.* Baku: Azerbaijan State Publications House, 1958.
Ayvazyan, Argam. *The Historical Monuments of Nakhichevan.* Translated by Kirkor H. Maksoudian. Detroit: Wayne State University Press, 1990.
Azerbaijani Poetry: Classic, Modern, Traditional. Edited by Mirza Ibrahimov. Moscow: Progress Publishers, 1969.
During, Jean. *La Musique Traditionnelle de l'Azerbayjan et la Science des Muqams.* Baden-Baden: V. Koerner, 1988.
Gink, Karoly. *Azerbaijan Mosques, Turrets, Palaces.* Budapest: Corvina Kiado, 1979.
Hajybaiov, Uzeiir. *Principles of Azerbaijani Folk Music.* Translated by G. Bairamov. Baku: Yazichi, 1985.
Mamedov, Farid. *Azerbaijan: Fortresses, Castles.* Baju: Interturan, 1994.
Smith, Michael G. "Cinema for the 'Soviet East': National Fact and Revolutionary Fiction in Early Azerbaijani Film." *Slavic Review* 6, no. 4 (Winter 1997): 645–679.

Description and Travel

Akchurin, Marat. *Red Odyssey: A Journey through the Soviet Republics.* New York: HarperCollins, 1992.
Azerbaijan: Land of Fire. Sherman Oaks, Calif.: Azerbaijan International, 1996.
Richards, Susan. *Epics of Everyday Life: Encounters in a Changing Russia.* New York: Viking, 1991.

Economics and Energy

Azerbaijan: From Crisis to Sustained Growth. Washington, D.C.: World Bank, 1993.

Azerbaijan: An Economic Profile. Washington, D.C.: Document Expedition Project, Library of Congress, 1995.

Croissant, Cynthia. *Azerbaijan, Oil, and Geopolitics.* Cornmack, N.Y.: Nova Science Publishers, 1998.

Daniloff, Ruth. "Waiting for the Oil Boom." *Smithsonian* 28, no. 10 (January 1998): 24–35.

Habib, Edgard H. *High Stakes Energy Game: Rebirth of Central Asian and Transcaucasian Oil and Gas Industries.* Washington, D.C.: WEFA Group, 1994.

Mehta, Vinod. *Soviet Economy: Development of Azerbaijan.* New Delhi: Sterling, 1982.

Tolf, R. W. *The Russian Rockefellers: The Saga of the Nobel Family and the Russian Oil Industry.* Stanford, Calif.: Stanford University Press, 1976.

Welsher, Lale Larissa. *Privatisation in Previously Centrally Planned Economies: The Case of Azerbaijan, 1991–1994.* New York: P. Lang, 1997.

World Bank. *Poverty Assessment.* Washington, D.C.: World Bank, 1997.

World Bank. *Statistical Handbook: States of the Former USSR: Studies of Economies in Transformation.* Washington, D.C.: World Bank, 1996.

Ethnic Relations

Central Asia and Transcaucasia: Ethnicity and Conflict. Edited by Vitaii Naumkin. Westport, Conn.: Greenwood Press, 1994.

Chinn, Jeff. *Russians As the New Minority: Ethnicity and Nationalism in the Soviet Successor States.* Boulder, Colo.: Westview Press, 1996.

Henze, Paul B. *The Transcaucasus in Transition.* Santa Monica, Calif.: RAND, 1991.

Kushen, Robert. *Conflict in the Soviet Union: Black January in Azerbaidzhan.* New York: Human Rights Watch, 1991.

Mansurov, Arif. *Blank Spaces of History and Perestroika.* Baku: Sharg-Garb Publishers, 1991.

Smith, Graham. *The Nationalities Question in the Post-Soviet States.* New York: Longman Group, 1996.

Transcaucasian Boundaries. Edited by John F. Wright, et al. New York: St. Martin's Press, 1996.

United States. Department of State. *Human Rights Report for Azerbaijan.* Washington, D.C.: Department of State, 1996.

History

Afary, Janet. "Peasant Revolution of the Caspian Region during the Iranian Constitutional Revolution, 1906–1909." *International Journal of Middle East Studies* 23, no. 2 (May 1991): 137–152.

Alstadt, Audrey. *The Azerbaijani Turks: Power and Identity under Russian Rule.* Stanford, Calif.: Hoover Institution Press, Stanford University, 1992.

————. "Azerbaijan Moves toward the Latin Alphabet." *RFE/RL Report on the USSR* 2, no. 29 (1990): 24–28.

————. "Muslim Workers and the Labor Movement in Pre-War Baku." In *Turkic Culture: Continuity and Change,* edited by S. M. Akural. Bloomington: Indiana University Press, 1987.

Atabaki, Touraj. *Azerbaijan: Ethnicity and Autonomy in Twentieth-Century Iran.* London: British Academy Press, 1993.

Baddeley, J. F. *The Russian Conquest of the Caucasus.* London: Longmans, Green & Co., 1908.

Bennigsen, Alexandre. *La presse et le mouvement national chez les musulmans de Russie avant 1920.* Paris: Mouton, 1964.

Bennigsen, Alexandre, and Endres Wimbusch. *Muslim National Communism in* the Soviet Union: A Revolutionary Strategy for the Colonial World. Chicago: Chicago University Press, 1979.

Bournoutian, George. *Eastern Armenia in the Last Decades of Persian Rule, 1807–1828: A Political and Socio-economic Study of the Khanate of Erivan on the Eve of the Russian Conquest.* Malibu, Calif.: Udena Publications, 1982.

Central Asia and the Caucasus after the Soviet Union: Domestic and International Dynamics. Edited by Mohiaddin Mesbahi. Gainesville: University of Florida Press, 1994.

Fawcett-L'Estrange, L. *Iran and the Cold War: The Azerbaijan Crisis of 1946.* New York: Cambridge University Press, 1992.

Gokay, Bulent. "The Battle for Baku: A Peculiar Episode in the History of the Caucasus." *Middle Eastern Studies* 34, no.1 (January 1998): 30–51.

Goltz, Thomas. *Azerbaijan Diary: A Rogue Reporter's Adventures in an Oil-Rich, War-Torn, Post-Soviet Republic.* Armonk, N.Y.: M. E. Sharpe, 1998.

———. *Requiem for a Would-Be Republic: The Rise and Demise of the Former Soviet Republic of Azerbaijan: A Personal Account of the Years 1991–1993.* Istanbul: Isis Press, 1994.

Hovannisian, Richard. *Armenia on the Road to Independence, 1918.* Berkeley, Calif.: University of California Press, 1969.

Kazemzadeh, Feridun. *The Struggle for Transcaucasia (1917–1921).* New York: Philosophical Library, 1951.

Leeuw, Charles van der. *Azerbaijan: A Quest for Identity.* New York: St. Martin's Press, 1998.

Manz, Beatrice. *The Rise and Role of Tamerlane.* Cambridge: Cambridge University Press, 1989.

Nissman, D. B. *The Soviet Union and Iranian Azerbaijan: The Use of Nationalism for Political Penetration.* Boulder, Colo.: Westview, 1987.

Rohrlich, A. A. "The 'Ali Bayramov Club,' the Journal 'Sharg Gadini,' and the Socialization of Azeri Women, 1920–1930." *Central Asian Survey* 5, no. 3/4 (1986): 221–240.

Rossow, R. "The Battle of Azerbaijan, 1946." *Middle Eastern Journal* 10 (Winter 1956).

Suny, Ronald G. *The Baku Commune, 1917–1918: Class and Nationality in the Russian Revolution.* Princeton, N.J.: Princeton University Press, 1972.

———. "Transcaucasia: Cultural Cohesion and Ethnic Revival in a Mutinational Society," pp. 228–253. In *The Nationalities Factor in Soviet Politics and Society,* edited by L. Hajda and M. Beissinger. Boulder, Colo.: Westview, 1990.

Swietochowski, Tadeusz. "The Himmat Party: Socialism and the Nationality Question in Russian Azerbaijan, 1904–1920." *Cahiers du monde russe et sovietique* 19 (1978): 119–142.

———. *Russian Azerbaijan, 1905–1920: The Shaping of National Identity in a Muslim Community.* New York: Cambridge University Press, 1985.

———. *Russia and Azerbaijan: A Borderland in Transition.* New York: Columbia University Press, 1995.

Teague-Jones, Reginald. *The Spy Who Disappeared: Diary of a Secret Mission to Russian Central Asia in 1918.* London: Gollancz, 1990.

Transcaucasia, Nationalism, and Social Change: Essays in the History of Armenia, Azerbaijan, and Georgia. Edited by Ronald Grigor. Ann Arbor, Mich.: University of Michigan Press, 1996.

Zenkovsky, S. *Pan-Turkism and Islam in Russia.* Cambridge, Mass: Harvard University Press, 1960.

Nagorno-Karabagh

Croissant, Michael P. *The Armenian–Azerbaijan Conflict: Causes and Implications.* Westport, Conn.: Praeger, 1998.

Fraser, Niall, Keith W. Hipel, John Jaworsky, and Ralph Zuljan. "A Conflict Analysis of the Armenian–Azerbaijan Dispute." *Journal of Conflict Resolution* 34, no. 4 (December 1990): 652–678.

Human Rights Watch. *Azerbaijan: Seven Years of Conflict in Nagorno-Karabakh.* New York: Human Rights Watch, 1994.

The Karabagh File: Documents and Facts on the Questions of Mountainous Karabagh, 1918–1988. Edited by G. Libaridian. Cambridge: Zoryan Insititute, 1989.

Rieff, David. "Case Study in Ethnic Strife." *Foreign Affairs* 76, no. 2 (March–April 1997): 118–133.

Saroyan, Mark. "The 'Karabakh Syndrome' and Azerbaijani Politics." *Problems of Communism* 39, no. 5 (September–October, 1990): 14–40.

Politics and Government

Bremmer, Ian A. *Nations and Politics in the Soviet Successor States.* Cambridge: Cambridge University Press, 1993.

Dawisha, Karen, and Bruce Parrott. *Conflict, Cleavage, and Change in Central Asia and the Caucasus.* New York: Cambridge University Press, 1997.

Hunter, Shireen T. *Transcaucasia in Transition: Nation-Building and Conflict.* Washington, D.C.: Center for Strategic and International Studies, 1994.

Kechichian, Joseph A., and Theodore W. Karasik. "The Crisis in Azerbaijan: How Clans Influence the Politics of an Emerging Republic." *Middle East Policy* 4, no. 1 (September 1995): 57–62.

Relations with Russia

Dima, Nicholas. "Russia, the Caucasus, and Chechenya." *The Journal of Social, Political and Economic Studies* 20, no. 2 (Summer 1995): 151–162.

Henze, Paul B. "Russia and the Caucasus." *Studies in Conflict and Terrorism* 19, no. 4 (October–December 1996): 389–401.

Lapidus, Gail W. "Gorbachev's Nationalities Problem." *Foreign Affairs* 68, no. 4 (Fall 1989): 92–119.

Mark, David E. "Eurasia Letter: Russia and the New Transcaucasus." *Foreign Policy* 105 (Winter 1996): 141–160.

Odom, William E., and Robert Dujaric. *Commonwealth or Empire? Russia, Central Asia, and the Transcaucasus*. Indianapolis: Hudson Institute, 1995.

Swietochowski, Tadeusz. *Russia and Azerbaijan: A Borderland in Transition*. New York: Columbia University Press, 1995.

Religion

Bennigsen, Alexandre, and Chantal Lemercier-Quelquejay. *Islam in the Soviet Union*. New York: Praeger, 1967.

Bennigsen, Alexandre, and Marie Broxup. *The Islamic Threat to the Soviet Union*. New York: St. Martin's Press, 1983.

Kolarz, Walter. *Religion in the Soviet Union*. London: Mac Millan, 1962

Social Studies

Gris, Henry. *May You Live to be 200*. South Brunswick, N.J.: A. S. Barnes, 1978.

Public Education in Soviet Azerbaijan: Appraisal of an Achievement. Edited by R. Avakov and A. Atakishiev. Paris: UNESCO, International Institute for Educational Planning, 1984.

Tohidi, Nayereh. "Soviet in Public, Azeri in Private: Gender, Islam, and Nationality in Soviet and Post-Soviet Azerbaijan." *Women's Studies International Forum* 19, nos. 1–2 (January–April): 111–125.

Works in Non-Western Languages

Akademiia Nauk Azerbaidzhanskoi SSSR, Baku. *Istoriia Azerbaidzhana*. Baku: Akademiia Nauk Azerbaidzhanskoi SSR, 1958–1963.

Aliyarli, S. *Azarbaycan tarixi*. Baku: 1996.

Bagirova, I. S. Politicheskie partii i organizatsii Azerbaidzhana v nachale XX veka. Baku: Elm, 1997.

Istoricheskaia geografiia Azerbaidzhana. Glavnyi redakor Z. M. Buniatov. Baku: Izd-vo "Elm," 1987.

Fedorov, Iu. *Kaspiiskaia neft i mezhdunarodnaia bezopastnost': Analitich-eskii doklad po materialam mezhdunarodnoit konferentsii.* Moscow: 1996.

Hasanli, Cemil. Azerbaycan tarihi, 1918–1920: Turkiyenin yardimindan Rusyanin isgaline kadar. Ankara: 1998.

Nasibzade, N. *Bolunmus Azarbaycan, butov Azarbaycan.* Baku: Ay-Ul-duz Nasriyyati, 1997.

Shorokhov, V. *Neft i politika Azerbaidzhana.* Moscow: Tsentr mezh-dunarodnykh Issledovanii, 1997.

About the Authors

Tadeusz Swietochowski is a professor of Russian and Middle Eastern history at Monmouth University. He has published over thirty articles and two books on Azerbaijan, including *Russia and Azerbaijan: A Borderland in Transition* (Columbia University Press, 1995), which has been translated into several languages. He is a member of the Columbia University Caspian Project and a consultant to the Sorosz Foundation and the Amoco and Frontera oil companies.

Brian C. Collins earned his M.A. in history from Monmouth University. His career has included work in museum fields; currently he is executive director of the Cedar Falls Historical Society. His book *Cedar Falls* was published in 1998 (Arcadia Press).